Alan Inglis was Called to the Bar of England and Wales in 1989 and the Scots Bar in 2009. He practices in both jurisdictions but primarily in Scotland. He has appeared in many of the leading cases which are considered in this book. He has always practiced exclusively in Family Law, particularly public law children's cases. Before that he was a social worker in Inner London specialising in child protection and mental health.

Alan is based at Arnot Manderson Advocates in Edinburgh and 4PB in London. He is a trustee of both the Scottish Child Law Centre and of the Equality Network, and also a Fellow of the International Academy of Family Lawyers.

A Practical Guide to Permanence Orders in Scotland

A Practical Guide to Permanence Orders in Scotland

Alan Inglis
MA, LL.M, FRSA
Advocate and Barrister
Arnot Manderson Advocates, Edinburgh
4PB, London

With a foreword by
The Rt Hon Lady Wise LL.D
A Senator of the College of Justice
Scotland

Law Brief Publishing

Published 2023 by Law Brief Publishing, an imprint of Law Brief Publishing Ltd
30 The Parks
Minehead
Somerset
TA24 8BT

www.lawbriefpublishing.com

Paperback: 978-1-914608-99-5

To the memory of

My Long Suffering Parents

FOREWORD BY THE RIGHT HON LADY WISE

I hope that practitioners will welcome this accessible text on Permanence Orders in Scotland by Alan Inglis as a long overdue addition to their legal library. Since their incipience, the legitimacy, scope and evidential basis for such orders have all been hotly contested. The rather convoluted test in the legislation creating them has required elucidation by the UK Supreme Court and the relationship between a Permanence Order and other less radical interventions in the lives of children is not always well understood.

The text sets out in a methodical and straightforward way the basic structure of a Permanence Order, the conditions that must be satisfied, the application process and its progress through court. Each of these is signposted by clear headings for ease of reference by the busy practitioner. The highlighted differences between sheriff court and Court of Session procedure will be of particular assistance to those who find themselves litigating in a less familiar forum. There are helpful tips on skilled witnesses in the evidence chapter and every family lawyer will benefit from having to hand the excellent chapters on threshold criteria and welfare when preparing a Permanence Order case. The vexed question of when authority to adopt can be included in the order is analysed constructively and the section on appeals includes a refresher on the limits of appellate jurisdiction that is of general application.

Throughout this concise yet admirably informative and comprehensive book the author makes suitable and effective reference to the significant body of case authorities that have fleshed out an understanding of the statutory provisions. Alan Inglis' experience as an advocate qualified to practice in both Scotland and England & Wales has enabled him to distil his encyclopaedic knowledge of the law and practice into an eminently readable text. I have no hesitation in commending it to the profession.

Morag Wise
April 2023

PREFACE

This slim volume arose out of a talk I was invited to give on the subject to Sheriffs at the Judicial Institute of Scotland. It was kind of Sheriff Matt Jackson KC to suggest that I covert it into this form and I hope the product does not cause embarrassment.

I am grateful to Lady Wise for her generous foreword and to Sheriff Wendy Sheehan for her helpful comments on an earlier draft. Any errors are my sole responsibility.

I have sought to state the law as at the feast day of St Agnes of Montepulciano (20th April 2023).

I am grateful to the solicitors who have entrusted to me their cases in this area of Scots Law. Jennifer Davidson, Alison Falconer, Gayle Heeps, Ross Mackenzie, Joanna MacPherson, Claire Anne McFadden, Nicola McLaren, Mona Reid, Eleanor Richards, Chris Thomson, Julia Walker, Karen Wilkie.

Alan Inglis
April 2023

CONTENTS

TABLE OF CASES

CHAPTER ONE

INTRODUCTION

The Adoption and Children (Scotland) Act 2007 which introduced Permanence Orders to Scotland follows the recommendations of the Adoption Policy Review which was established by the Scottish Executive in 2001 and reported in 2005.[1]

The orders proposed were designed to replace two orders then available which the Review judged not adequately to meet children's best interests where they could not safely be cared for in their birth families. Firstly, children could be 'freed for adoption' under section 18 Adoption (Scotland) Act 1978. The effect of such an order was to extinguish the parental rights and responsibilities of the birth parents without transferring them to any other persons. The Review also identified that such an order might remain in force even though the child was not ultimately adopted because they could not be replaced by other orders maintaining the child in care. Additionally, they contained no mechanism for the maintenance of contact between the child and their birth family.

Secondly, a local authority might apply for a Parental Responsibilities Order under section 86 Children (Scotland) Act 1995. The order transferred all parental responsibilities to the applicant local authority whereas the Review considered it desirable that a court should be able to consider that some such responsibilities should remain with the birth family. There was no ability to transfer aspects of parental responsibility to long term substitute carers. There was no provision which enabled a

---

1 *Adoption: Better Choices for Our Children. Report of Phase II* Adoption Policy Review Group, Scottish Executive June 2005

person whose parental responsibilities had been removed to apply for contact if they were not in a position to seek the revocation of the order.

Foster parents had no formal role in either of these legal regimes. Long term carers could only apply for private law orders for parental rights and responsibilities and residence under section 11 Children (Scotland) Act 1995. Such an order would terminate the involvement of the local authority and therefore any allowances which enabled the care to be provided.

The Review therefore recommended the introduction of a Permanence Order which would authorise the local authority which obtained it to regulate the child's residence and to 'control, direct and guide' the child. The court should then be able to consider whether the birth parent(s) could retain some aspect of parental rights and responsibilities which would be shared with the local authority. In addition, the court should determine whether and if so to what extent the child should continue to have contact which their parent(s). The order should be sufficiently flexible to enable the court to vest aspects of parental responsibility in the child's long-term carers.

The different criteria which existed for the making of the old orders would be replaced by a single threshold for the grant of a Permanence Order, namely that either the child had no one who was exercising parental responsibilities or parental rights, or that, where there was such a person, the child's residence with them would be 'seriously detrimental' to their welfare.

The Review recommended that the court should be empowered on the application of the local authority to grant authority for the child to be adopted. This would require either that every person with parental responsibilities and rights agrees, cannot be found or is incapable of giving agreement, or the child's welfare requires agreement to be dispensed with. There should be provision for contact orders to be made which would endure until the making of any adoption order.

An explicit objective of the proposed measures was the avoidance of delay in the determination of the futures of children who cannot be cared for at home. Research in 2018 found that it had not had that effect to any significant degree.[2] The harmful effect of delay on children continues to attract criticism from the higher courts.[3] Section 30 Children (Scotland) Act 2020 inserted into section 14 of the 2007 Act a requirement for the court to "have regard to any risk of prejudice to the child's welfare that delay in proceedings would pose." Identical amendments were inserted into the Children (Scotland) Act 1995 and the Children's Hearings (Scotland) Act 2011. Section 14 of the 2007 Act applies only to the adoption provisions of the Act. It appears to be a drafting error which inserts this requirement in all children's proceedings except permanence. Harmful delay is avoided if courts faithfully adhere to the timescales in the rules which are considered in Chapter three.

As long ago as 1992 the Inner House in *Lothian RC v A*[4] observed:

> "It is essential, especially in a small court where judicial resources are already under pressure for other reasons, that the sheriff should be given at the outset a carefully considered forecast of the time which the proof is expected to take. With the benefit of that information arrangements can and should be made for the sheriff to be released from other duties so that he can give priority to the case without interruption and until it has been completed by the issuing of his interlocutor. Special arrangements of that kind are clearly necessary if the sheriff is to

---

2 Hanson, Henderson and Kurlus "Adoption and permanence planning in Scotland: Impact of the Adoption and Children (Scotland) Act 2007 on key processes and timescales" *Child and Family Social Work* 2018 1-8

3 *TW v Aberdeenshire Council* [2012] CSIH 37; *S v L* 2012 UKSC 30; *North Lanarkshire v KR* 2018 CSIH 59; *City of Edinburgh Council v DG* 2019 SC 1.

4 1992 SLT 858 at 862

> maintain the continuity of thought throughout the proceedings which is so necessary to a proper disposal of the case."

This book is intended as a practitioner's guide. The statutory drafting of the Act which implemented the recommendations of the Adoption Policy Review has been the subject of frequent judicial criticism. It is often obscure and unnecessarily complex. This offers challenges to those required to implement its provisions and it is hoped that this study will assist.

The structure of this book seeks to take the reader chronologically through the permanence process from inception to conclusion. Chapter Two examines what the proposed order consists of; Chapter Three describes the application process including pre-action requirements; Chapter Four considers the manner in which evidence might be presented; Chapters Five and Six describe what must be proved before an order can lawfully be made; Chapter Seven looks at the law relating to post order contact in the context of the differences between Permanence Orders and those to which Authority to Adopt is attached. Chapter Eight examines the potential liabilities for expenses and Chapter Nine considers appeals.

CHAPTER TWO

THE STRUCTURE OF A PERMANENCE ORDER

In this chapter I describe and explain the orders which are available in sections 80-84 Adoption and Children (Scotland) Act 2007. I have cross-referred to the identified provisions in the Children (Scotland) Act where they arise in order to obviate the need created in the statute to jump between texts.

The Orders

A Permanence Order comprises two and in some cases three, components. Each refers back to the parental rights and responsibilities identified in sections 1 and 2 of the Children (Scotland) Act 1995. A Permanence Order will therefore comprehensively allocate each of these attributes of parenthood. Section 80 (3) of the 2007 Act requires that "in making a permanence order in respect of a child, the appropriate court must secure that each parental responsibility and parental right in respect of the child vests in a person."

Section 81 of the 2007 Act provides that the mandatory provisions within a permeance order are:

(a) the responsibility mentioned in section 1(1)(b)(ii) of the 1995 Act (provision of guidance appropriate to child's stage of development) in relation to the child, and

(b) the right mentioned in section 2(1)(a) of that Act (regulation of child's residence) in relation to the child.

Section 87 confirms that the making of a permanence order automatically terminates the right of any person holding the right of any parent or guardian of the child to determine the child's place of residence and therefore precludes the sharing of that right by that person with the local authority.

The ancillary provisions are set forth in section 82 namely:

> (1) The ancillary provisions are provisions—
>
> (a) vesting in the local authority for the appropriate period—
>
> (i) such of the parental responsibilities mentioned in section 1(1)(a), (b)(i) and (d) of the 1995 Act, and
>
> (ii) such of the parental rights mentioned in section 2(1)(b) and (d) of that Act,
>
> in relation to the child as the court considers appropriate,
>
> (b) vesting in a person other than the local authority for the appropriate period—
>
> (i) such of the parental responsibilities mentioned in section 1(1) of that Act, and
>
> (ii) such of the parental rights mentioned in section 2(1)(b) to (d) of that Act,
>
> in relation to the child as the court considers appropriate,

(c) extinguishing any parental responsibilities which, immediately before the making of the order, vested in a parent or guardian of the child, and which—

 (i) by virtue of section 81(1)(a) or paragraph (a)(i), vest in the local authority, or

 (ii) by virtue of paragraph (b)(i), vest in a person other than the authority,

(d) extinguishing any parental rights in relation to the child which, immediately before the making of the order, vested in a parent or guardian of the child, and which—

 (i) by virtue of paragraph (a)(ii), vest in the local authority, or

 (ii) by virtue of paragraph (b)(ii), vest in a person other than the authority,

(e) specifying such arrangements for contact between the child and any other person as the court considers appropriate and to be in the best interests of the child, and

(f) determining any question which has arisen in connection with—

 (i) any parental responsibilities or parental rights in relation to the child, or

 (ii) any other aspect of the welfare of the child.

Parental Rights and Parental Responsibilities

Subsection (a) enables the court to vest in the local authority the parental responsibilities set out in the specified parts of section 1 and the rights set out in section 2 Children (Scotland) Act 1995 namely:

1 Parental Responsibilities

(1) (…)

(a) to safeguard and promote the child's health, development and welfare;

(b) to provide, in a manner appropriate to the stage of development of the child—

(i) direction;

to the child;

(c) (…)

(d) to act as the child's legal representative,

2 Parental Rights

(1) (…)

(a) (…)

(b) to control, direct or guide, in a manner appropriate to the stage of development of the child, the child's upbringing;

(c) (…)

(d) to act as the child's legal representative.

Subsection (1) (b) enables the court to vest in a person other than the local authority the following rights and responsibilities:

1. Parental Responsibilities

(1) (...)

(a) to safeguard and promote the child's health, development and welfare;

(b) to provide, in a manner appropriate to the stage of development of the child—

(i) direction;

(ii) guidance,

to the child;

(c) if the child is not living with the parent, to maintain personal relations and direct contact with the child on a regular basis; and

(d) to act as the child's legal representative,

2. Parental Rights

(1) (...)

(a) (...)

(b) to control, direct or guide, in a manner appropriate to the stage of development of the child, the child's upbringing;

(c) if the child is not living with him, to maintain personal relations and direct contact with the child on a regular basis; and

(d) to act as the child's legal representative.

Sub-section (1) (c) allows to court to extinguish any parental rights which vest in the local authority because of the mandatory provision of the permanence order or which vest in a person other than the local authority after an order made under subsection (b) above.

Subsection (1) (d) allows the court to extinguish any parental rights of a parent or guardian which now vest in either the local authority or any person other than the local authority under subsections (a) or (b) above.

An order under subsection 1 (e) "specifying such arrangements for contact between the child and any other person" is an order which can only be made in favour of a natural person.[5]

Subsection 83 (2) is difficult to interpret. Permanence orders may only be made to endure for "the appropriate period" Section 83 (2) provides:

> In subsection (1), *"the appropriate period"* means—
>
> (a) in the case of the responsibility mentioned in section 1(1)(b)(ii) of the 1995 Act, the period beginning with the making of the permanence order and ending with the day on which the child reaches the age of 18,
>
> (b) in any other case, the period beginning with the making of the permanence order and ending with the day on which the child reaches the age of 16.

---

5 *East Lothian Council Petrs* [2012] CSIH 3

This appears to mean that a permanence order may only last until sixteen except in the respect of the parental responsibility it imposes on the local authority to provide guidance to the child under subsection (1) above. If, however, the child is aged sixteen when the order is sought the mandatory provision cannot be made and this would negate the purpose of the order.

Conditions

The conditions which must be satisfied before a Permanence Order can lawfully be made are set out in section 84 of the Act:

> (1) Except where subsection (2) applies, a permanence order may not be made in respect of a child who is aged 12 or over unless the child consents.
>
> (2) This subsection applies where the court is satisfied that the child is incapable of consenting to the order.
>
> (3) The court may not make a permanence order in respect of a child unless it considers that it would be better for the child that the order be made than that it should not be made.
>
> (4) In considering whether to make a permanence order and, if so, what provision the order should make, the court is to regard the need to safeguard and promote the welfare of the child throughout childhood as the paramount consideration.
>
> (5) Before making a permanence order, the court must—
>
> > (a) after taking account of the child's age and maturity, so far as is reasonably practicable—

(i) give the child the opportunity to indicate whether the child wishes to express any views, and

(ii) if the child does so wish, give the child the opportunity to express them,

(b) have regard to—

(i) any such views the child may express,

(ii) the child's religious persuasion, racial origin and cultural and linguistic background, and

(iii) the likely effect on the child of the making of the order, and

(c) be satisfied that—

(i) there is no person who has the right mentioned in subsection (1)(a) of section 2 of the 1995 Act to have the child living with the person or otherwise to regulate the child's residence, or

(ii) where there is such a person, the child's residence with the person is, or is likely to be, seriously detrimental to the welfare of the child.

(6) A child who is aged 12 or over is presumed to be of sufficient age and maturity to form a view for the purposes of subsection (5)(a).

The section embodies the importance which Scots Law attaches to children's rights. Section 84 (1) operates as a bar on the making of a permanence order if a competent child over the age of 12 does not consent to it being made. Subsection (2) sets out a presumption of capacity which can only be displaced by proof of the contrary. Given the absolute bar on the making of an order if the child is competent any further process in the application is otiose and the issue should be resolved immediately evidence of unless incapacity is available.

As the Inner House has repeatedly observed, and as will be examined more fully in Chapter 5, the remainder of the section is poorly drafted because the starting point of the process of determining whether to make a Permanence Order is the threshold criterion is buried in section 84 (5) (c) (ii) – the "serious detriment" test.[6]

Authority to Adopt

At the same time as making a Permanence Order, the court may include the grant of authority to adopt if an application for such an order has been included in the application for the Permanence Order. This bears significant similarities to the previous orders which freed children for adoption under section 18 Adoption (Scotland) Act 1978. The effect of the authority is to extinguish the parental responsibilities and parental rights of the parent or guardian without transferring them to adopters who are not parties to the applications.

Before considering whether to grant authority to adopt the court must have satisfied itself that the threshold for making a Permanence Order under section 84 (5) (c) (ii) has been established.[7]

The applicable part of the statute is section 83 of the Act:

> (1) The conditions referred to in section 80(2)(c) are—

6 *TW v Aberdeenshire Council* [2012] CSIH 37; *KR v Stirling Council* [2016] CSIH 36.

7 *East Lothian Council Petrs* 2011 Fam LR 80

(a) that the local authority has, in the application for the permanence order, requested that the order include provision granting authority for the child to be adopted,

(b) that the court is satisfied that the child has been, or is likely to be, placed for adoption,

(c) that, in the case of each parent or guardian of the child, the court is satisfied—

(i) that the parent or guardian understands what the effect of making an adoption order would be and consents to the making of such an order in relation to the child, or

(ii) that the parent's or guardian's consent to the making of such an order should be dispensed with on one of the grounds mentioned in subsection (2),

(d) that the court considers that it would be better for the child if it were to grant authority for the child to be adopted than if it were not to grant such authority.

(2) Those grounds are—

(a) that the parent or guardian is dead,

(b) that the parent or guardian cannot be found or is incapable of giving consent,

(c) that subsection (3) or (4) applies,

(d) that, where neither of those subsections applies, the welfare of the child otherwise requires the consent to be dispensed with.

(3) This subsection applies if the parent or guardian—

(a) has parental responsibilities or parental rights in relation to the child other than those mentioned in sections 1(1)(c) and 2(1)(c) of the 1995 Act,

(b) is, in the opinion of the court, unable satisfactorily to—

(i) discharge those responsibilities, or

(ii) exercise those rights, and

(c) is likely to continue to be unable to do so.

(4) This subsection applies if—

(a) the parent or guardian has, by virtue of the making of a permanence order which does not include provision granting authority for the child to be adopted, no parental responsibilities or parental rights in relation to the child, and

(b) it is unlikely that such responsibilities will be imposed on, or such rights given to, the parent or guardian.

As in section 84, the starting point of the Court's review is placed towards the end of the section. The authority to adopt may be granted if the parent consents or her consent is dispensed with on a ground set forth in subsection (2). These include that the parent or guardian in dead, cannot be found or is incapable of consenting. It would be unusual of these grounds to be considered in the context of an application for a Permanence Order with Authority to Adopt as they would more expeditiously be features of a direct petition for adoption.

The grounds for dispensation more likely to be considered are those set out in subsections (2) (c) and (d), (3) or (4).

Subsection 2 (d) permits consent to be dispensed with where "the welfare of the child otherwise requires the consent to be dispensed with". Subsection 2 (c) however, provides that this ground may only be relied upon if neither of subsections (3) or (4) applies. It is therefore necessary to consider whether they do apply before it is legitimate to rely on the welfare ground in subsection (2) (d).

The Adoption Policy Review recommended that there should be a single ground of dispensation on the foundation that the child's welfare. The Scottish Parliament considered that this was an insufficiently exacting test and inserted the text now found at subsection (3). This does not, however, achieve the desired effect because resort to the straightforward welfare test is always available if the apparently more stringent "incapacity test" is not established.

As drafted the section appears to require the court to be satisfied on evidence that the incapacity requirement does not apply in each individual case. There is no authority for the proposition that the parties, or the applicant alone, could concede that the incapacity threshold does not apply and therefore proceed directly to the welfare ground alone.

Subsection (4) applies where a permanence order made previously did not contain authority to adopt and the birth parents had been deprived of their parental responsibilities and parental rights and the court is satisfied that those responsibilities and rights would be unlikely to be imposed upon them.

Once the court is satisfied that a ground for dispensing with parental consent to adoption exists in the case it is then required to consider the matters set out in subsections (1) (b) – that the child is likely to be place for adoption – and (1) (d) that it is better for the child to grant authority to adopt than not to grant it.

Further consideration specific to Authority to Adopt

When determining whether to grant authority to adopt the court is "coming to a decision relating to the adoption of a child" and it is therefore required to consider the matters set forth in section 14 (2) – (4) of the Act:[8]

> (1) Subsections (2) to (4) apply where a court or adoption agency is coming to a decision relating to the adoption of a child.
>
> (2) The court or adoption agency must have regard to all the circumstances of the case.
>
> (3) The court or adoption agency is to regard the need to safeguard and promote the welfare of the child throughout the child's life as the paramount consideration.
>
> (4) The court or adoption agency must, so far as is reasonably practicable, have regard in particular to—
>
> > (a) the value of a stable family unit in the child's development,
> >
> > (b) the child's ascertainable views regarding the decision (taking account of the child's age and maturity),
> >
> > (c) the child's religious persuasion, racial origin and cultural and linguistic background, and
> >
> > (d) the likely effect on the child, throughout the child's life, of the making of an adoption order.

---

8 *Aberdeenshire Council Ptrs* 2011 SLT (Sh Ct) 186; *S v Edinburgh City Council* 2013 Fam LR 2

These must be addressed having regard to the principles of necessity and proportionality.[9]

The Effect of a Permanence Order

By section 87 of the 2007 Act a Permanence Order extinguishes the parental right to have the child living with them which was held by a parent or guardian immediately before the order was made.

Section 88 provides that the making of a Permanence Order has the effect of revoking any existing order made under section 11 of the Children (Scotland9 Act 1995.

9 *AV v AJF* 2017 Fam LR 110 at para 82

CHAPTER THREE

THE APPLICATION

Local Authority Statutory Pre-Application Duties

There are no regulations governing the process within a local authority leading to an application for a Permanence Order without authority to adopt. There is no power devolved to the Scottish Ministers in Part 2 of the 2007 Act to promulgate such regulations.

A local authority is required by section 17 of the Children (Scotland) Act 1995 in relation to any child looked after by it to:

(1)(a) safeguard and promote his welfare (which shall, in the exercise of their duty to him be their paramount concern)

(b) (…)

(c) take such steps to promote, on a regular basis, personal relations and direct contact between the child and any person with parental responsibilities in relation to him as appear to them to be, having regard to their duty to him under paragraph (a) above, both practicable and appropriate; and

(d) take such steps to promote, on a regular basis, personal relations and direct contact between the child and any person mentioned in subsection (1A) as appear to them to be appropriate having regard to their duty to the child under paragraph (a).

In making any decisions in relation to that duty it is required by section 17 (3) to have regard to the ascertainable wishes of the child, his parents and any other person with parental rights, any sibling, any "any other person with whom the child has lived and with whom the child has an ongoing relationship with the character of a relationship between siblings", and any other person whom the authority considers to be relevant."

Section 17 (4) provides that in making any decision in relation to the child to have regard to:

(a) to the views (if he wishes to express them) of the child concerned, taking account of his age and maturity;

(b) to such views of any person mentioned in subsection (3)(b) to (d) above as they have been able to ascertain; and

(c) to the child's religious persuasion, racial origin and cultural and linguistic background.

The Child's Plan

Regulation 3 Looked After Children (Scotland) Regulations 2009 require the local authority to make assessments of the child's needs including in paragraph "(g) whether the local authority should seek a change in the child's legal status". This is then a component of the "Child's Plan" under regulation 4.

The Child's Plan is then considered at the Looked After Children's Review held under regulations 44 (child placed with parents) or 46 (child placed away from parents). Regulation 44 (2) sets out the frequency with which such reviews are required to take place:

(a) a first review within 6 weeks of the placement;

(b) a second review within 3 months from the date of the first review; and

(c) thereafter subsequent reviews within 6 months from the date of the previous review.

Once a decision has been made in that forum that it is in the child's interest that an application in made for a Permanence Order there is no statutory instrument providing regulations as to how the matter is further considered within the local authority as required where the plane is for adoption. The Looked After Children Regulations (Scotland) 2009 at regulation 17 require the establishment of a 'fostering panel'. This is concerned with the functions set out in regulation 20 namely:

> (2) The fostering panel must make recommendations on the following matters:–
>
> > (a) whether a prospective foster carer is suitable or continues to be suitable to be a foster carer;
> >
> > (b) whether a prospective foster carer would be a suitable foster carer for–
> >
> > > (i) a particular child or children;
> > >
> > > (ii) any child; or
> > >
> > > (iii) certain categories of child;
> >
> > (c) the maximum number of children a particular foster carer may have in their care at any one time

It will be observed that these functions do not include consideration of the desirability of applications for statutory orders. In practice local authorities combine the functions of the fostering and adoption panels in a single Permanence and Adoption Panel whose responsibilities include the consideration of whether a Permanence Order would be likely to meet the child's needs. Furthermore, although not a legal requirement, the recommendation of that Panel is typically subject to the approval of the Agency Decision Maker.

Permanence Order with Authority to Adopt

All Scottish local authorities are adoption agencies by reason of the obligation to provide an adoption service which is set out in section 1 of the 2007 Act and section 119 which defines 'adoption agency' in terms of an adoption service. Where a LAAC Review resolves that an application should be made for a Permanence Order with Authority to Adopt it is 'considering adoption for a child' and the Adoption Agencies (Scotland) Regulations 2009 are engaged.

The local authority considering such an application is subject to multiple check lists identifying the factors which it must consider many of which are repetitious.

Firstly, the child concerned is almost certainly already looked after by the local authority which must take into account the matters set out in section 17 Children (Scotland) Act 1995 which were considered above.

Secondly, it is bound to examine the factors which are listed in regulation 12 of the Adoption Agencies (Scotland) Regulations:

> (1) This regulation applies where an adoption agency is considering adoption for a child.
>
> (2) The adoption agency must, so far as is reasonably practicable and in the child's best interests–
>
> (a) consult and take into account the views of–
>
> (i) the child, taking account of their age and maturity; and
>
> (ii) the child's parents and guardians if their whereabouts are known;

(b) take account of the child's religious persuasion, racial origin and cultural and linguistic background where known;

(c) obtain and record in writing the information in Parts II and III of Schedule 1;

(d) ensure that arrangements are made for the child to be examined by a registered medical practitioner; and

(e) obtain from the practitioner who has carried out the examination referred to in sub-paragraph (d) a written assessment of the child's health.

Finally, it is bound to address the contents of section 14 of the 2007 Act because it is an adoption agency "coming to a decision relating to the adoption of a child":

(1) Subsections (2) to (4) apply where a court or adoption agency is coming to a decision relating to the adoption of a child.

(2) The court or adoption agency must have regard to all the circumstances of the case.

(3) The court or adoption agency is to regard the need to safeguard and promote the welfare of the child throughout the child's life as the paramount consideration.

(4) The court or adoption agency must, so far as is reasonably practicable, have regard in particular to—

(a) the value of a stable family unit in the child's development,

(b) the child's ascertainable views regarding the decision (taking account of the child's age and maturity),

(c) the child's religious persuasion, racial origin and cultural and linguistic background, and

(d) the likely effect on the child, throughout the child's life, of the making of an adoption order.

(5) Where an adoption agency is placing a child for adoption it must have regard, so far as is reasonably practicable, to the views of the parents, guardians and other relatives of the child.

(6) In carrying out the duties imposed on it by subsections (2) to (4) an adoption agency must, before making any arrangements for the adoption of a child, consider whether adoption is likely best to meet the needs of the child or whether there is some better practical alternative for the child.

(7) If an adoption agency concludes that there is an alternative such as is mentioned in subsection (6), it must not make arrangements for the adoption of the child.

The Adoption Panel and the Agency Decision Maker

Once the Child's Care Plan includes a conclusion that adoption is in their best interests regulation 19 (3) Adoption Agencies (Scotland) Regulation 2009 requires that the case must be referred to the adoption panel providing the reports specified in regulation 19 (4).

The duties of the adoption panel are set out in regulation 6. They must consider the case of every child, proposed placement and prospective adopter. They must give recommendations on the following matters:

(a) whether adoption is in the best interests of the child;

(b) whether an application for a permanence order granting authority for the child to be adopted should be made under Section 80 of the Act;

(c) whether a prospective adopter is suitable or continues to be suitable to be an adoptive parent;

(d) whether a prospective adopter would be a suitable adoptive parent for a particular child; and

(e) any other matter referred to the adoption panel which is relevant to the adoption agency's functions under the Act.

If the Panel recommends that there should be continuing contact between the child and their parents it is required by regulation 6 (4) to provide a written report of its reasons for doing so.

The decisions of the Adoption Panel are recommendations only. The final arbiter is the agency decision maker, in practice the Chief Social Work Officer who is required by regulation 13 to take into account the decision of the Adoption Panel and to reach a concluded decision within 14 days of receiving it.

Compulsory Supervision Orders and Children's Hearing Advice

Most children about whom a local authority concludes should be the subject of an application for a Permanence Order with or without Authority to Adopt will already be subject to a Compulsory Supervision Order. Once the authority has completed the stages outlined above they must refer the matter to the Principal Reporter under section 131 Children's Hearings (Scotland) Act 2011 requiring a review of the Compulsory Supervision Order. It must do so *inter alia* if it intends either to make an application under section 80 of the 2007 Act or if it intends to place the child for adoption.

At that review, the Children's Hearing is required by section 141 of the 2011 Act to prepare a report containing advice about the circumstances of the child to the Court deciding the application under section 80 of the 2007 Act. The court hearing an application for a Permanence Order is obliged by section 89 of the 2007 Act to have regard to the contents of the report when determining whether to kame the order sought.

The Court

The "appropriate court" for applications under the 2007 Act is defined in section 118 of the Act. If the child is in Scotland, the appropriate court is either the Court of Session or the sheriff court of the sheriffdom in which the child is. Where the child is not in Scotland and the application is for either an adoption order or a permanence order with authority to adopt, the appropriate court is the Court of Session.

The sheriff court may transfer the petition to another sheriff court under rule 26.1 (1) Ordinary Cause Rules 1993 or remit to the Court of Session under section 92 Courts Reform (Scotland) Act 2014. Transfer between Sheriff Courts may be appropriate where the child is located in a foster placement distant from their family and/or the local authority whose witnesses will be required at proof. Rule 26 (1) (4) OCR specifically requires the court to have regard to "the convenience of the parties and their witnesses" when considering a motion to transfer an application to another court.

In *Midlothian Council, Petitioner*[10] Sheriff Holligan remitted to the Court of Session a permanence order application issued in the Edinburgh Sheriff Court although the child was in another sheriffdom. He held that the power to remit was available despite that court not having jurisdiction to adjudicate on the substantive application. The case of *Mullan v*

[10] 2012 Fam LR 25

Anderson[11] establishes that the sheriff's power to remit to the Court of Session is not limited to cases of importance and difficulty. An example of where remit to the Court of Session is appropriate is where there are extant proceedings relating to the child in that court as in *Campbell v Campbell.*[12]

The Application

An application for a Permanence Order may only be made by a local authority.[13] 'Local authority' is defined in section 119 of the Act as "a constituted under section 2 of the Local Government (Scotland) Act 1994 which would preclude an application by a local authority in another jurisdiction which had placed a child in Scotland.

There is a situation in which a local authority, each of which is an adoption agency created by section 1 of the 2007 Act, is required to make an application for a Permanence Order. Where such an agency proposes to make arrangements for the adoption of a child who is not the subject of a Compulsory Supervision Order and whose parents have not consented to those arrangements the agency must apply for a permanence order with authority to adopt.[14] The application must be made within 28 days of formal notification by the parent of their opposition or of the agency's resolution to proceed without such formal notification.

Before issuing any application for a Permanence Order the local authority will consider whether to seek a serial number which prohibits the disclosure of the child' address "to any person whose consent to the making of the order is required" (rule 67.37 RCS; rule 43 Sheriff Court

11 1993 SLT 835

12 1960 SLT (Notes) 20

13 Section 80 (1) 2007 Act

14 Adoption Agencies (Scotland) Regulations 2009 reg 21

Adoption Rules 2009). In both courts the rules provide that on an application for the assignment of a serial number the relevant court officer must provide one. The phrasing of the rules does not permit the court to exercise any discretion in relating to the assignment of a serial number to the petition.

The petition must be in Form 67.28 in the Court of Session or Form 11 in the Sheriff Court. In each case it must be accompanied by a report by the petitioner dealing with the multiple matters set out in Rule 67.28 (2) RCS or Rule 31 Sheriff Court Adoption Rules as the case may be.[15] In

---

15
i. how the needs of the child came to the notice of the petitioner;
ii. any relevant family circumstances of the child;
iii. a description of the physical and mental health of the child (including any special needs) and his emotional, behavioral and educational development;
iv. an account of the discussion by the petitioner with the parents or guardians of the child and, if appropriate, with the child about their wishes and the alternatives to a permanence order;
v. where appropriate, whether the father of the child has been given notice and provided with the prescribed information under section 105(2) of the 2007 Act;
vi. the knowledge of the petitioner of the position of other relatives or persons likely to be involved;
vii. an account of the search by the petitioner for any parent or guardian who cannot be found;
viii. the arrangements of the petitioner to care for the child after the making of a permanence order (including the arrangements for contact between the child and any other person);
ix. the child's religious persuasion, racial origin and cultural and linguistic background;
x. the likely effect on the child of the making of a permanence order;

either case, if the report is not available at the time of lodging the court should pronounce an interlocutor requiring the petitioner to prepare and lodge the report within two weeks or such other time as the court may allow.

Court rules – preliminary

On receipt of the petition the court must appoint a curator *ad litem,* and in respect of a petition which seeks authority to adopt, a reporting officer (rule 67.29 RCS; rule 32 Sheriff Court Adoption Rules 2009). The duties of the curator *ad litem* and the reporting officer are extensive and are contained in rule 67.38 RCS and rule 44 Sheriff Court Adoption Rules 2009.[16] The reporting officer is required to witness the signature of a

---

xi. whether there is a person who has the right mentioned in section 2(1)(a) of the 1995 Act to have the child living with the person or otherwise to regulate the child's residence and, where there is such a person, evidence that the child's residence with the person is or is likely to be seriously detrimental to the welfare of the child;

xii. whether the child is or has been married or a civil partner;

xiii. in the case of a petition containing a request that the order include provision granting authority for the child to be adopted, the matters mentioned in paragraph (3);

xiv. in the case of a petition in respect of a child who is aged 12 or over, whether the child consents to the making of the order or is incapable of doing so;

xv. whether the child is subject to a supervision requirement under section 70 of the 1995 Act;

xvi. any other information which may be of assistance to the court having regard, in particular, to sections 83 (if appropriate) and 84 of the 2007 Act;

16 a. have regard to safeguarding the interests of the child as his paramount duty;

child over the age of 12 where they consent to the making of the order sought.

On the lodging of the petition the court must fix a hearing on the by order rule or a preliminary hearing between 6 and 8 weeks from the date of lodging. (rule 67.29 (2) RSC; rule 33 (1) (a) Sheriff Court Adoption Rules 2009).

---

b. inquire, so far as he considers necessary into the facts and circumstances stated in the petition or minute, as the case may be, and in any report lodged under rule 31(2)(b);

c. where appropriate, establish the child's religious persuasion, racial origin and cultural and linguistic background;

d. where appropriate, establish whether the order is likely to safeguard and promote the welfare of the child throughout childhood;

e. ascertain whether the child is subject to a supervision requirement under section 70 of the 1995 Act;

f. ascertain from the child whether he wishes to express a view and, where the child indicates his wish to express a view, ascertain that view;

g. ascertain the likely effect on the child of the making of the order;

h. where appropriate, ascertain whether it would be better for the child that the order be made than that it should not be made;

i. where appropriate, ascertain whether it would be better for the child if the court were to grant authority for the child to be adopted than if it were not to grant such authority;

j. where appropriate, ascertain whether the child has been, or is likely to be, placed for adoption.

Intimation

The rules identifying to whom intimation must be given are contained respectively in rule 67.30 (1) (b) – (e) and (2) RCS and rule 33 (1) (a) – (e) and (2) Sheriff Court Adoption Rules 2009. They rules distinguish between petitions which seek authority to adopt and those which do not. In relation to the latter the rules provide that:

(b) where the petition does not contain a request that the order include provision granting authority for the child to be adopted, the petitioner must intimate a copy of the petition along with a notice of intimation in Form 67.30-A to—

(i) any person who has parental responsibilities or parental rights in relation to the child; and

(ii) any person who claims to have an interest;

Rule 67.30 (2) RCS and Rule 33 (2) Sheriff Court Rules 2009 identify to whom intimation is required where the petition seeks Authority to Adopt namely:

(a) every person who can be found and whose consent to the making of the order is required to be given or dispensed with under the 2007 Act;

(b) if no such person can be found, a relative of the child within the meaning of section 119(1) of the 2007 Act unless the address of such a relative is not known to the petitioner and cannot reasonably be ascertained.

In the case of such a petition intimation is also required by on:

(c) (ii) the father of the child if he does not have, and never has had, parental responsibilities and parental rights in relation to the child;

Responses to intimation and Statement of Facts

In the Sheriff Court, a person upon whom intimation has been effected is required by rule 34 Sheriff Court Adoption Rules 2009 to lodge a form of response in Form 15 and intimate it to the petitioner within 21 days of intimation of the petition on them. Thereafter, the petitioner is required by rule 34A to lodge and intimate on the other parties a 'brief' statement of the facts upon which they intend to rely in particular (in what appears to be reverse chronological order):

(a) considerations under section 14 of the 2007 Act;

(b) ancillary provisions under section 82 of the 2007 Act;

(c) conditions under section 83 of the 2007 Act;

(d) conditions and considerations under section 84 of the 2007 Act.

Case management

The hearing on the By Order rule in the Court of Session and the Preliminary Hearing in the Sheriff Court are governed respectively by rule 67.31 and rule 35. They enable the court to make dispose of the cause if no party has indicated and intention to oppose the petition. Where the petition is opposed the rules require that the court to:

(i) ascertain from the parties the anticipated length of any proof that may be required;

(ii) fix a diet of proof not less than 12 and not more than 16 weeks after the date of the hearing on the By Order Roll unless, on cause shown, a longer period is appropriate;

(iii) give such directions as to the preparation for the proof as it considers appropriate;

(iv) order answers and any other documents to be lodged within 21 days of the date of the hearing on the By Order Roll or such other period as it considers appropriate.

The effect of this rule, together with the six to eight weeks from the lodging of the petition required before the By Order or Preliminary Hearing is that the proof is required to take place within six months of the lodging of the petition unless a longer period is appropriate. The construction of the rule would indicate that what is 'appropriate' must relate to the particular feature of the case which the court is considering and not other factors and not administrative convenience.

In addition the rules provide at (3) that the court may:

(a) if it is not satisfied that the facts stated in the petition are supported by the documents lodged with it or by the reports of the curator ad litem and reporting officer, order the production of further documents; and

(b) where it considers it appropriate to do so, fix a pre-proof hearing not less than 2 and not more than 6 weeks before the diet of proof;

(c) make such other order as it considers appropriate for the expeditious progress of the case.

The requirement of expedition which is set out in this and other rules emphasises that these are petitions which are intended to be concluded within a timescale which does not cause unnecessary harm to the child by delaying decisions about their future.

Pre-Proof Hearing

The final stage before proof is the pre-proof hearing which is described in rule 67.32 RCS and rule 36 Sheriff Court Adoption Rules. These provide that:

(1) If the court appoints a pre-proof hearing under rule 67.31, the parties must provide the court with sufficient information to enable it to conduct the hearing as provided for in this rule.

(2) At the pre-proof hearing the court must ascertain, so far as is reasonably practicable, whether the cause is likely to proceed to proof on the date fixed for that purpose and, in particular, the court must consider—

(a) the state of preparation of the parties;

(b) the extent to which the parties have complied with any orders made by the court under rule 67.31.

(3) At the pre-proof hearing the court may—

(a) discharge the proof and fix a new date for such proof;

(b) adjourn the pre-proof hearing;

(c) order the lodging of joint minutes of agreement, affidavits and expert reports within such period as it considers appropriate;

(d) make such other order as it considers appropriate to secure the expeditious progress of the cause.

The significance of paragraph (3) (d) of the rule in preventing the lengthening of proceedings by the prolix presentation of cases has been repeatedly emphasised in appellate courts. In *B v G* [17] the Supreme Court held per Lord Reed at paragraph 34:

> "In particular, contrary to the impression conveyed by some of the submissions in the present case, the sheriff's role at a proof is not confined to ruling on objections and otherwise sitting impassively in silence. He possesses the power to intervene to discourage prolixity, repetition, the leading of evidence of unnecessary witnesses and the leading of evidence on matters which are unlikely to assist the court to reach a decision."

In *RG v Glasgow City Council* [18] it was held that the effect of the rule was that:

> It is for the sheriff to ascertain what issues are in dispute (rule 35(1)(b)(i)). Thereafter it is entirely a matter for the discretion of the sheriff to determine what requires proof (r 36(3)(b) and what evidence, whether oral, documentary or otherwise, he or she wishes to hear in order to resolve such issues as he or she considers ought to be addressed before determining whether the statutory tests have been met, and with what effect.

A particular example of the application of the rule will be further considered in Chapter 4 which deals with evidence.

[17] 2012 SC (UKSC) 293

[18] 2020 SC 1

Decision and judgement in the Sheriff Court

In the Sheriff Court, rule 38 Sheriff Court Adoption Rules 2009 sets out the obligations of the Sheriff at and following the conclusion of the proof. There is no corresponding rule in the Court of Session. The significant provisions of the rule are:

> (1) At the conclusion of the proof the sheriff may—
>
> > (a) pronounce a decision; or
> >
> > (b) reserve judgment.
>
> (2) If the sheriff pronounces his decision at the end of the proof, he—
>
> > (a) must state briefly the grounds of his decision, including the reasons for his decision on any questions of law or of admissibility of evidence; and
> >
> > (b) may, and if requested to do so by one of the parties must, append to the interlocutor a note setting out those matters and his findings in fact and law.
>
> (3) If the sheriff pronounces his decision after reserving judgment, he must give to the sheriff clerk within 4 weeks of the conclusion of the proof—
>
> > (a) an interlocutor giving effect to his decision and incorporating findings in fact and law; and

Interim Orders

The need for interim orders may arise at any point during the pendency of the petition. They do so in two distinct processes.

Section 97 of the 2007 Act authorises the court seized of an application for a Permanence Order to "make such interim order as it thinks fit". In *Dumfries and Galloway Council, Petitioners*[19] Sheriff K A Ross observed that such an order may be sought by any party with an interest in the proceedings or *ex proprio muto;* that it might competently reflect terms which might otherwise be included in a Compulsory Supervision Order such as contact; that section 86 of the Act permitted the respondents to the application to make representations; that the court did not require to be satisfied that the threshold test in section 84 (5) (c) was satisfied and that the court must consider the best interests of the child before making any interim order.

Dumfries and Galloway was a case in which a direct application for an interim order under section 97 was made to the court. More nuanced issues arise where the Children's Hearing has previously made a report to the court under section 95 of the Act. There are superficially conflicting sheriff court decisions considering how the court should respond.

Section 95 of the 2007 Act provides that where the application for a Permanence Order has not been determined and the Children's Hearing proposes to make or vary a Compulsory Supervision Order they must prepare a report for the Court seized of the Permanence Order application.

Upon receipt of a report under section 95, by rule 51 (2) Sheriff Court Adoption Rules 2009 and rule 67.43 RCS the court must send a copy of the report to:

---

[19] 2012 SLT (Sh Ct) 173

(i) the parties to the application;

(ii) any relevant person in relation to the child within the meaning given by section 93(2) of the 1995 Act; and

(iii) such other person as the court considers appropriate.

Section 96 then provides:

(2) A compulsory supervision order may not be made or varied (other than by interim variation, as defined in section 140 of the Children's Hearings (Scotland) Act 2011 (asp 1)) in respect of the child, until the application is determined (or, as the case may be, withdrawn or abandoned).

(3) Subsection (2) does not apply if the court to which the application is made refers the child's case to the Principal Reporter (whether following receipt of a report of a report under section 95 or otherwise)

The first case which considered this provision was the decision of Sheriff K Mackie in *City of Edinburgh Council. Petitioners (No 1).* [20] The Sheriff held at paragraph 10 that:

> In terms of s 97 of the 2007 Act a court may make such interim order as it thinks fit and if the provisions of the order conflict or are inconsistent with a supervision requirement the provisions of the order prevail. In these circumstances and taken together with the prohibition against the making or modification of a supervision requirement during proceedings, in my opinion, it is a reasonable interpretation of ss 95, 96 and 97 that Parliament intended that the court should be the principal forum for

[20] 2010 Fam LR 89

making decisions in relation to the child during the process of determining an application for a permanence order.

She therefore declined to make any reference to the Principal Reporter under section 96 (3) of the Act.

A different interpretation was made by Sheriff Holligan in *City of Edinburgh Council, Petitioners*[21] He agreed that whilst a permanence order is being considered the court was the principal forum for making decisions in relation to the child. He further held the effect of section 96 (2) and (3) is that if the court before which the application for a Permanence Order is pending receives such a report it may refer that matter to the Principal Reporter and the prohibition in subsection (2) on making or varying the Compulsory Supervision Order no longer applies. In that case Sheriff Holligan further held that "where a children's hearing has made a proposal to vary the terms of a supervision requirement, if the court does refer the matter to the principal reporter then the children's hearing will be limited to consideration of the proposal which was the subject of the report to the court." Given the proximity to the proof he declined to refer the matter back to the Principal Reporter.

A more straightforward approach to addressing the need for interim arrangements for the child is available under section 97 of the 2007 Act. Its use further avoids the undesirable prospect of two fora simultaneously exercising jurisdiction over the same child.[22]

There are other pragmatic considerations which favour the direct motion under section 97 over the section 95 report. The former requires a single court hearing. The latter involves two hearings at the Children's Hearing and one in court. The parties are invariably all publicly funded. The

21 2011 Fam LR 83

22 2012 SLT (Sh Ct) 173

direct motion avoids significant unnecessary delay and demands on the public purse.

In *Shetland Islands Council, Applicant*[23] the Reporter had inadvertently allowed the Compulsory Supervision Order to lapse together with the provision within it which gave legal authority for the child's placement with foster parents. They had deferred a decision on making a CSO at the same time as they made a report to the Sheriff under section 95. The Sheriff held that, as there was no longer a CSO he could not make a referral to the Principal Reporter under section 96 (3). He therefore made an interim order under section 97 requiring the child to remain in her foster placement.

Section 97 (2) empowers the appropriate court to "make such order as it thinks fit." The court must also discharge the CSO under section 97 (3) if "it would no longer necessary for the protection, guidance treatment or control of the child."

By subsection (5) (b) of section 97, if "the provisions of the interim order or are otherwise inconsistent with the Compulsory Supervision Order the provisions of the interim order prevail."

An application for an Interim Order must be made by motion in either court by rule 67.44 RCS and rule 52 Sheriff Court Adoption Rules 2009.

Revocation of the Compulsory Supervision Order

Section 89 of the 2007 Act allows the court to revoke a Compulsory Supervision Order on making a Permanence Order. The section reads:

(1) Subsection (2) applies where—

23 2017 SLT (Sh Ct) 59

(a) the child in respect of whom a permanence order is to be made is subject to a [compulsory supervision order , and

(b) the appropriate court is satisfied that, were it to make a permanence order in respect of the child, it would no longer be necessary that, for the protection, guidance, treatment or control of the child, the child be subject to the compulsory supervision order.

(2) The court must make an order providing that, on the making of the permanence order, the [compulsory supervision order ceases to have effect.

It is therefore mandatory to revoke the order if the conditions in section 89 (1) are established. The effect of this provision was considered in *Edinburgh City Council v L*[24] Lady Wise observed at paragraph 65 that:

> "There may have been a tendency to alight on subsection (2) of section 89 which requires revocation of a CSO on the making of a permanence order without appreciating that that is mandated only where, in terms of section 89(1)(b) of the 2007 Act , the court is satisfied that continuation of the CSO is no longer necessary for the protection, guidance, treatment or control of the child. Accordingly, the issue in every case must first be whether the court is so satisfied."

The Compulsory Supervision Order was discharged in that case and there is no report of a case in which a Permanence Order was made and the CSO not discharged. It remains to be seen in what circumstances it would be necessary to make a Permanence Order if the continuation of

[24] 2021 CSOH 24

the CSO was necessary for the protection, guidance, treatment or control of the child."

The continuation of the Compulsory Supervision Order inhibits the exercise by the local authority of the powers vested in them by the Permanence Order. Section 90 of the 2007 Act provides that:

> (1) Subsection (2) applies where a local authority has, by virtue of a permanence order, parental responsibilities or parental rights in relation to a child.
>
> (2) The local authority must not act in any way which would be incompatible with—
>
> > (a) (...)
> >
> > (b) any [compulsory supervision order or interim compulsory supervision order to which the child is subject.

Section 67 (2) Children's Hearings (Scotland) Act 2011 lists the Grounds of Referral which may invoke the jurisdiction of the Children's Hearing. These include at 67 (2) (i):

> (i) a permanence order is in force in respect of the child and special measures are needed to support the child.

This, however, is after the CSO has previously been discharged and would only allow the Hearing to make "special measures" which are not defined in that Act. They may include secure accommodation authorisation and a movement condition under section 83 of that Act. The terms of this provision indicate the limited interplay which Parliament intended between the Children's Hearing and the local authority in which the Permanence Order is vested.

Variation

Although not part of the initial permanence process described above and hereafter, it is convenient at this stage to consider the other types of order provided for in Part 2 of the 2007 Act each of which relates to Permanence Orders which are extant. They are variation, amendment and revocation.

The first such application is for variation of ancillary provisions in the order under section 92 of the Act. Section 92 (2) allows the court to 'vary such ancillary provisions as the court considers appropriate.' No further criteria are identified in the section. Section 99 of the Act requires the local authority to apply for a variation if there has been a material change in circumstances and 'in consequence of that change to order ought to be varied".

Those enabled to apply for variation are listed in section 92 (3). They are:

- (a) the local authority on whose application the permanence order was made,
- (b) if the child in respect of whom the order was made is—
  - (i) aged 12 or over, or
  - (ii) under the age of 12 but, in the court's opinion (taking account of the child's age and maturity), capable of understanding the effect of the order, that child,
- (c) any person in whom parental responsibilities and parental rights are vested by virtue of the order,
- (d) any person in whom were vested, immediately before the making of the order, any parental responsibilities or

parental rights which, by virtue of the making of the order, vest in another person,

(e) any person in whom were vested, immediately before a variation by virtue of this section of the order, parental responsibilities or parental rights which, by virtue of the variation, vest in another person,

(f) any other person who claims an interest.

In the Court of Session the application is commenced by note (rule 67.34 RCS) and in the Sheriff Court by minute (rule 40 Sheriff Court Adoption Rules 2009), The relevant rules identify the information which must be set out in the application.

Amendment

Amendment is the process by which authority to adopt is added to a Permanence Order which was granted without such provision. It is provided for in section 83 of the 2007 Act. The application may only be made by the local authority by virtue of subsection 83 (2) and may be granted if and only if:-

(a) the court is satisfied that the child has been placed for adoption, or is likely to be placed for adoption,

(b) the court is satisfied that the condition in subsection (3) or subsection (4) is met, and

(c) the court considers that it would be better for the child that authority for the child to be adopted is granted than that it should not be granted.

Subsection (3) applies where the parent or guardian consents and subsection (4) applies the criteria in section 83 which have been set out above.

The application for such amendment must be made by note in the Court of Session (rule 67.35 RCS) and minute in the Sheriff Court (rule 41 Sheriff Court Adoption Rules 2009).

Revocation is dealt with in section 98 of the 2007 Act. Section 98 (2) allows the application for revocation to be applied for by the local authority on whose application the permanence order was made, and any person affected by the order who has obtained the leave of the court. By section 98 (1) the court must consider all the circumstances of the case in particular:-

(a) a material change in the circumstances directly relating to any of the order's provisions,

(b) any wish by the parent or guardian of the child in respect of whom the order was made to have reinstated any parental responsibilities or parental rights vested in another person by virtue of the order.

Section 98 (3) provides that subsections (4) (5) (a) and (b) and (6) of section 84 apply to the revocation of a permanence order as they apply to the making of such an order. It is unclear why the court is not directed to consider whether the original threshold criteria under section 84 (5) (c) continues to apply. This may be because the drafters failed to appreciate the significance of the section in the way in which the judiciary has.

Where leave is required it is sought by motion under rule 67.41 RCS and minute under rule 48 Sheriff Court Adoption Rules. In both courts the motion or minute is not to be intimated in the first instance. In the court of session the court may hear the applicant and either refuse the application or make such order as is appropriate prior to determination. In the Sheriff Court the sheriff is to consider the application without hearing from the applicant and may refuse it or require the applicant to intimate it on such persons as the sheriff considers appropriate. If any person upon whom intimation is ordered wishes to be heard they must notify the court within 14 days and a hearing will then be scheduled.

In *R v Angus Council*[25] leave was refused where there was no evidence of any change of circumstances although the procedure adopted by the Sheriff does not appear to have conformed to the summary process envisaged by the rules.

If the Court orders the revocation of the permanence order, section 100 allows the court to substitute a section 11 order:-

> (2) The court must consider whether to make an order under section 11 of the 1995 Act—
>
> > (a) imposing on a person specified in the order parental responsibilities in relation to the child, and
> >
> > (b) giving to such a person parental rights in relation to the child.

[25] 2010 GWD 40-806

CHAPTER FOUR

EVIDENCE

Form

The primary form of evidence in Permanence proceedings is affidavit. It remains in the court's discretion whether to order affidavit evidence. In the Court of Session rule 67.19 (4) allows the court to "order the lodging of joint minutes of agreement, affidavits, expert reports and any other documents within such period as it considers appropriate.." In the Sheriff court at the preliminary hearing the sheriff is required by rule 18 (1) (b) (iii) to "consider the scope for the use of affidavits and other documents in place of oral evidence."

Practice Notes issued in 2009 in all Sheriffdoms with the exception of Glasgow and Strathkelvin apply to all proceedings under the 2007 Act are in common form. They describe the status of such evidence:

> "It should be noted that evidence may be presented in the form of affidavits or other written documents (Civil Evidence (Scotland) Act 1988, section 2; McVinnie -v- McVinnie 1995 SLT (Sh Ct) 81; Glaser -v- Glaser 1997 SLT 456). The sheriff is bound to consider reports placed before him or her even if the authors are not called to speak to them, and the strict rules of evidence do not apply (T, Petitioner 1997 SLT 724 at 730L). Such considerations may render the attendance of certain witnesses unnecessary; although for other reasons it may be preferable to call the author of a document. The parties should therefore apply their minds to the question whether any evidence might be appropriately presented in the form of an affidavit or other document and the sheriff should encourage them to decide that question at the pre-proof hearing. The sheriff should also encourage the use of affidavits to cover

> noncontentious (or indeed contentious) issues where that would save the time of witnesses and the court. Notwithstanding that an affidavit has been lodged, its author may be called to give evidence at the proof (see paragraph 3 of the judgment of Lady Smith in Petitions of Aberdeenshire Council to declare A, B and C free for adoption, Court of Session, 22 June 2004).

Affidavits must conform to the accepted rules of evidence. It is the evidence of the deponent standing in place of their oral evidence.

Documentary evidence in the form of productions, usually social work files, is typically lodged voluntarily by the local authority petitioners. Where this is thought to be incomplete it is important that any respondents proceed by way of specification of documents under rule 28 Ordinary Causes Rules. In *In the Matter of XY Council*[26] a respondent applied to the council as a Subject Access Request under the Data Protection Act 2018. The council was the required by the General Data Protection Regulation to redact the documents removing references to all third parties. The court held that the proper course was to recover a full social work file by obtaining an interlocutor compelling disclosure of unredacted files.

Relevance

The fundamental rule that to be admissible evidence must be relevant to the issue which the court is required to determine has not always been understood in children's cases. In *B v G*[27] the Supreme Court was concerned with a child contact dispute in which the Sheriff Court proof lasted 52 days over one year. It is stretching credulity to suggest that such

26 2020 Fam LR 148

27 2012 SC (UKSC) 293

a narrow dispute could produce such a volume of evidence which is relevant.

The definition of relevance is set out in *Strathmore Group Ltd v Credit Lyonnais*[28] per Lord Osborne at 1031 G – I:

> First, the ultimate test of the relevancy of averment or evidence is whether the material in question has a reasonably direct bearing on the subject under investigation. In any particular case, there could come a point at which it would be possible for the court to say that the bearing of some fact was too indirect and too remote properly to assist in deciding the issue in question. Secondly, in my opinion it is apparent that expediency has a part to play in reaching a decision as to what averment or evidence may be held to be relevant, and what not. Accordingly, judicial discretion is involved to that extent in deciding upon the point at which averments or evidence must properly be excluded as irrelevant."

Views of the Child

Given the importance attached by Scots Law generally and the 2007 Act in particular it is appropriate to consider first how that evidence enters the court process. The curator's duties are set out in rule 67.38 RCS and rule 44 Sheriff Court Adoption Rules 2009. As noted in the previous chapter the curator is appointed immediately upon the lodging of the petition. In (3) (f) in both rules the curator if directed to "ascertain from the child whether he wishes to express a view and, where the child indicates his wish to express a view, ascertain that view."

Rule 67.40 RCS and rule 46 Sheriff Court Adoption Rules 2009 then allow the court to "order such procedural steps to be taken as it considers

28 1994 SLT 1023,

appropriate to ascertain the views of the child." Having received responses to those procedural steps the court may require any views in writing to be held in a sealed envelope not available to any other person[29]

Whilst the rule provides that the views are confidential there are obvious Article 6 issues if they remain so. In *Re D (Minors) (Adoption Reports: Confidentiality)*[30] the House of Lords held at 615D:

> "It is a fundamental principle of fairness that a party is entitled to the disclosure of all materials which may be taken into account by the court when reaching a decision adverse to that party. (....) Non-disclosure should be the exception and not the rule. The court should be rigorous in its examination of the risk and gravity of the feared harm to the child and should order non-disclosure only when the case for doing so is compelling."

The same approach is evident in the decision of the European Court of Human Rights in *McMichael v UK*[31] in which a breach of Article 8 was found where the parents were denied access to reports upon which the Children's Hearing based their decision to make orders which placed their son in care.

The private law case of *Shields v Shields*[32] is clear that the views considered must be contemporaneous with the making of the order. There is no principled reason why this should differ in the public law orders considered here. Clearly, there are practical challenges where applications are subject to delay and the children would be exposed to repeated questioning about their wishes.

---

29 RCS rule 67.40 (2) and rule 40 (2) Sheriff Court Adoption Rules.

30 [1995] 4 All ER 385

31 [1995] SC 31

32 2002 SC 246

Also in the private law context, section 11 (7) Children (Scotland) Act 1995 requires that the "court shall so far as practicable– (i) give him an opportunity to indicate whether he wishes to express his views". Section 84 (5) (a) of the 2007 Act similarly provides that the court must take account of the child's view "so far as is reasonably practicable. In *M v C* [33] the Inner House held that what is practicable had to be considered in the context of the court's requirement to act in the child's best interests. At paragraph 10 it was observed that "if a court is ordered to treat the best interests of a child as paramount, and also to do something concerning the child if it is practicable, it does little if any violence to that wording to decide not to do that something if it violates the first instruction."

The weight which should be attached to the views of a child will vary from case to case. In the context of public law applications the facts which are said to demonstrate serious detriment may themselves compromise a child's capacity to identify their own best interests.

Children's evidence

Generally it is understood that children being required to give evidence in court proceedings is inimical to their welfare. The Scottish Court Service, *Evidence and Procedure Review* observed:

> '2.1 It is now widely accepted that taking the evidence of young and vulnerable witnesses requires special care, and that subjecting them to the traditional adversarial form of examination and cross-examination is no longer acceptable. This is for two main reasons. The first is that, as has been known for some time, the experience of going to court and recounting

---

[33] 2021 SC 324

> traumatic events is especially distressing for children, and can cause long-term damage …
>
> 2.3 The second reason is that, particularly for young and vulnerable witnesses, traditional examination and cross-examination techniques in court are a poor way of eliciting comprehensive, reliable and accurate accounts of their experience'.

In *S v Children's Reporter*[34] the Inner House decided that where the case against the parents depended solely upon the hearsay accounts in Joint Investigative Interviews of the children, the court was required to consider "sufficiently weighty counterbalancing factors which permitted a proper assessment of the children's evidence." These could include permitting direct questioning of the children by the parents' representatives subject to suitable vulnerable witness measures.

This follows the Supreme Court case of *Re W*[35] which eschewed any presumption that children should not give evidence in family proceedings but held[36]

> "The essential test is whether justice can be done to all the parties without further questioning of the child. Our prediction is that, if the court is called upon to do it, the consequence of the balancing exercise will usually be that the additional benefits to the court's task in calling the child do not outweigh the additional harm that it will do to the child. A wise parent with his child's interests truly at heart will understand that too."

---

34 2017 SC 31

35 [2010] 1 WLR 701

36 At [30}

In *NM v Children's Reporter*[37] the Sheriff Appeal Court emphasised the passage in *S*, which in turn adopted ECrtHR decisions:

> "It will not necessarily be unfair to admit an untested statement in the absence of the witness but reliance on a statement which cannot be tested raises a question about fairness which the court requires to determine by reference to the answers to three questions: Was there good reason for the absence of the witness? Was the hearsay statement led in his place the sole or decisive reason for the decision in question? Were there counterbalancing factors which compensated for such handicaps as the admission of untested evidence gave rise to? The answer to any one of these questions will not in itself be determinative."

Such an analysis is inevitably case specific, in the instant case the impugned evidence was decisive but not the sole evidence. The countervailing factors were that (i) the appellant had not insisted on the attendance of the relevant witness; (ii) the sheriff had regard to other available evidence : (iii) the court had views two JII's of the witness in one of which she made allegations which she retracted in the second; (iv) the appellants solicitors had availed themselves of the opportunity to preconize the witness; and the appellant had the opportunity to give evidence himself. In all the circumstances the hearing was fair.

Where it is intended by any party that a child should give evidence in any civil proceedings they must follow the procedure set out in section 12 Vulnerable Witness (Scotland) Act 2004. Before the hearing at which the evidence is to be lead, the court must make an order either authorising the use of special measures or that the child witness is to give evidence without such measures.[38]

---

37 2018 Fam LR 19

38 Section 1 Vulnerable Witness (Scotland) Act 2004.

The party seeking to adduce the evidence of a child witness must lodge with the court a 'vulnerable witness notice' either specifying the special measures they deem appropriate or stating that they consider that the child should give evidence without such measures.[39] The special measures are listed in subsection (3) and are:

(a) the use of a live television link in accordance with section 20 where the place from which the child witness is to give evidence by means of the link is another part of the court building in which the court-room is located,

(b) the use of a screen in accordance with section 21, or

(c) the use of a supporter in accordance with section 22 in conjunction with either of the special measures referred to in paragraphs (a) and (b) above,

The court may only permit the child giving evidence without special measures either if they agree and the court is satisfied it is appropriate or one of the grounds in subsection 4 (b) applies:

(i) the use of any special measure for the purpose of taking the evidence of the child witness would give rise to a significant risk of prejudice to the fairness of the proceedings or otherwise to the interests of justice, and

(ii) that risk significantly outweighs any risk of prejudice to the interests of the child witness if the order is made.

Chapter 45 Ordinary Causes Rules sets out the procedure which must be followed in applications relating to child witnesses. The vulnerable witness notice must be intimated to the other parties. The court may

[39] Section 2 Act of 2004

make the order without a hearing; may require further information or fix a hearing. In the Court of Session the process is set out in rule 35A RSC.

Skilled witnesses

The term 'skilled witness' refers to those persons who are entitled by their possession of a body of expert knowledge to give opinion evidence in a court. The presentation of evidence from witnesses purported experts is commonplace in applications for Permanence Orders. Typically these will be psychologists or former social workers.

The Practice Notes previously referred to record at paragraph 22:

> "The sheriff should discourage the unnecessary use of expert witnesses. If expert evidence is essential, the sheriff should encourage the joint instruction of a single expert by all parties. If one party instructs an expert report, it should be disclosed to the other parties with a view to the agreement of as much of its contents as possible."

In the Sheriff Court rule 35 requires the sheriff to address at the preliminary hearing "what, if any, expert evidence is required and consider the scope for joint instruction of a single expert."

There is no obligation on the applicant for a Permanence Order to lead expert evidence of the impact on children of being returned to the care of their parents. It is a matter for the court on the available evidence.[40]

[40] Fife Council v KPM 2019 SLT (Sh Ct) 32

The limits on the role of the expert in providing evidence to the Court were addressed in *Davie v Magistrates of Edinburgh*[41] by Lord President (Cooper):

> "Expert witnesses, however skilled or eminent, can give no more than evidence. They cannot usurp the functions of the jury or Judge sitting as a jury, any more than a technical assessor can substitute his advice for the judgment of the Court (...) the parties have invoked the decision of a judicial tribunal and not an oracular pronouncement by an expert."

A classic and succinct statement of this function is found in the case of *R v Turner*[42] "an expert's opinion is admissible to furnish the court with scientific information which is likely to be outside the experience and knowledge of a judge or jury."

The decision of the Supreme Court of *Kennedy v Cordia*[43] is of singular significance in understating the role of expert evidence in Scottish courts. At paragraph 44 the court set out the four core requirements of admissible expert evidence:

> "There are in our view four considerations which govern the admissibility of skilled evidence: (i) whether the proposed skilled evidence will assist the court in its task; (ii) whether the witness has the necessary knowledge and experience; (iii) whether the witness is impartial in his or her presentation and assessment of the evidence; and (iv) whether there is a reliable body of knowledge or experience to underpin the expert's evidence. All four considerations apply to opinion evidence, although, as we state below, when the first consideration is applied to opinion evidence the threshold is the necessity of such evidence. The four

---

41 1953 SC 34 at page 49

42 [1975] QB 834 at 842

43 2016 (UKSC) 59

> considerations also apply to skilled evidence of fact, where the skilled witness draws on the knowledge and experience of others rather than or in addition to personal observation or its equivalent."

The relevance of these dicta to family law, first recognised by Sheriff Anwar (as she then was) in *Q v P*[44] has resulted in a series of cases in which the admissibility of such evidence has been challenged focussing on one of the grounds identifiable in the case.

Assisting the court

The court referred to the dicta in *R v Turner*[45] where it was held that "if on the proven facts a judge or jury can form their own conclusions without help, then the opinion of an expert is unnecessary." This principle is well recognised in Sottish children's cases. In *A v B and C*[46] the House of Lords held at 142:

> "In a case like this I think that a judge is well able to estimate the probable effect of uprooting a child of tender years and transferring it from adopting parents, with whom it is happy, to its natural parents, of whom it has no recollection. In unusual cases medical evidence may be helpful, but I should be sorry to see any general tendency to call medical evidence in these cases."

A similar observation was made by the Sheriff Appeal Court in the case of JA & TA and JC v Mr & Mrs AC[47]

> "The courts are familiar with judging what may or may not be in the best interests of children; absent some underlying or

[44] 2016 Fam LR 54

[45] [1975] QB 834

[46] 1971 SC (HL) 129

[47] 2018 Fam LR 75

> suspected psychological condition, or some unusual or exceptional factual matrix, the courts are generally well equipped to analyse and consider the likely reaction to or adjustment to a change in their circumstances, without the need for evidence from, in this case, a clinical psychologist."

In *Re W (A Child) (Adoption: Grandparents' Competing Claim),*[48] Sir Andrew MacFarlane P held at paragraph 66 that "where the relationship that the child has established with new carers is at the core of one side of the balancing exercise, the question of what harm, if any, the child may suffer if that relationship is now broken must be considered. The court will almost invariably require some expert evidence of the strength of the attachment that exists between the particular child and the particular carers and the likely emotional and psychological consequences of ending it." In *JA, TA, JC v Mr & Mrs AC*[49] the Sheriff Appeal Court rejected the need for psychological evidence of how children might transition from a settled placement to the care of their grandparents.

A particular example of the rejection of evidence which the court deemed to be unnecessary and therefore inadmissible is the case of *Q v P* in which Sheriff Anwar cited a further passage from *R v Turner* in which it was stated that "The fact that an expert witness has impressive scientific qualifications does not by that fact alone make his opinion on matters of human nature and behaviour within the limits of normality any more helpful than that of the jurors themselves".

Authorities emphasise the requirement that there must be an issue in the case which is within the professional expertise of the intended witness and outwith the experience of the Bench. In *Q v P* Sheriff Anwar observed that "in the absence of any factual basis for concluding or suspecting that a child is suffering from, or affected by, or is likely to be suffering from or affected by, an underlying psychological issue, requiring

48 [2017] 1 WLR 889

49 2018 Fam Lr 75

the input of a suitably qualified expert, the basis for appointing a child psychologist must be questionable." In *City of Edinburgh Council v EAH* [50] Sheriff Welsh QC rejected as unnecessary the evidence of an expert on the 'trustworthiness' of a potential carer because in the absence of "some unusual psychological pathology" he was not assisted by such evidence.

Expert evidence on the reliability of a witness who is not suffering from a diagnosed mental illness is inadmissible. This is clear from *Turner* at 842:

> "The jury had to decide what reliance they could put upon the defendant's evidence. He had to be judged as someone who was not mentally disordered. This is what juries are empanelled to do. The law assumes they can perform their duties properly. The jury in this case did not need, and should not have been offered, the evidence of a psychiatrist to help them decide whether the defendant's evidence was truthful."

The court does not require expert evidence on the law which is applicable in Scotland.[51]

It is under this heading that consideration requires to be given to the limits of any expert's evidence. It cannot be said to assist the court if it seeks to usurp the judge's function. This is clear from *Davie v Magistrates of Edinburgh:*[52]

> "Expert witnesses, however skilled or eminent, can give no more than evidence. They cannot usurp the functions of the jury or a judge sitting as a jury...Their duty is to furnish the judge or jury with the necessary scientific criteria for testing the accuracy of their own conclusions, so as to enable the judge or jury to form

---

[50] 2018 GWD 18-234

[51] D v Victim Support (Scotland) (No 2) 2019 Rep LR 15

[52] 1953 SC 34

> their own independent judgement by the application of these criteria to the facts proved in evidence…the decision is for the judge or jury"

The witness's knowledge and experience

In order to provide admissible evidence it must be demonstrated that the witness has the necessary qualifications and experience to assist the court. In *C v T*[53] objection was taken to an expert report on the ground *inter alia* that its authority lacked the necessary qualifications and experience. The court did not make a finding on that objection, having concluded that the report was inadmissible on the foundation that it was unnecessary.

A recent English decision[54] notes that 'psychologist' is not a protected status and that caution should be exercised in the instruction of an individual not a member of a relevant regulatory body, such as the Health and Care Professionals Council.

The impartiality of the witness

The requirement of impartiality similarly has a venerable history. It can be traced to *National Justice Compania Naviera SA v Prudential Assurance Company Limited (The Ikarian Reefer) (No 1)*[55] where it was held that the obligation is to "objective unbiased opinion in relation to matters which his expertise".

This is a feature of both admissibility and reliability. Thus in *A v A*[56] – a financial provision application – Lady Wise found in relation to expert valuation evidence that the witness "departed from the necessary position

---

53 2022 Fam LR

54 C (Parental Alienation: Instruction of Expert) [2023] EWHC 345 (Fam)

55 1993 2 Lloyds Rep 08

56 2020 Fam LR 95 at [32]

of impartiality of a witness giving opinion evidence and appeared to promote the defender's cause on valuation. His position in evidence was that he did not seek to defend all of his initial valuations. As I cannot accept his final figures I am effectively left with no definitive valuation by Mr Ranachan."

In *C v T*[57] Sheriff Andrew Mackie determined at inadmissible an expert report which was partial because the expert had failed to interview essential witnesses. That is the approach which emerges from the English authorities.[58] The case management powers available under the rules applicable to the 2007 Act enable this issue of the admissibility of an expert report to be addressed in advance of the proof.

Reliable body of knowledge or experience

This rarely poses a difficulty in permanence cases where appropriately qualified psychologists and social workers are held to possess a reliable body of knowledge and experience. In *Mearrns v Smedvig Ltd*[59] Lord Easie observed that "a party seeking to lead a witness with purported knowledge or experience outwith generally recognised fields would need to set up by investigation and evidence not only the qualifications and expertise of the individual skilled witness, but the methodology and validity of that field of knowledge or science.

The Expert Witness

Despite the terms of the Practice Note encouraging the exchange of expert reports, it is not unknown for a party to withhold from the court and the other parties the report of an expert instructed by them under a

---

57 2022 Fam LR 39

58 *Toth v Jarman* [2006] 4 All ER 1276

59 1999 SC 243

claim of confidentiality. As long ago as 1939 in the case of *Black v Bairds & Dalmellington*[60] the Inner House held that:

> "The modern tendency to relax the strictness of the older practice in the recovery of documents has been due to the anxiety of judges that the ascertainment of the truth should not be hampered by too great an insistence upon technical rules. If confidentiality is a plea of real substance it ought properly to be given effect to, but if, as sometimes happens, it is merely a pretext for concealing something that is inconvenient to be divulged, the plea ought to receive little consideration."

The position of a witness in such circumstances was considered in the case of *Harmony Shipping Co S.A. v Saudi Europe Line Ltd*[61], In that case a handwriting expert initially instructed by the claimant and subsequently advised the defendant. His opinion favoured the defendant who sought to subpoena him. The claimant objected on the ground that a witness could not advise one party and then give evidence for another. Giving the judgment of the Court Lord Denning MR held:

> "... the court is entitled, in order to ascertain the truth, to have the actual facts which he has observed adduced before it and to have his independent opinion on these facts ... there is no property in an expert witness as to the facts he has observed and his own independent opinion on them."
>
> "In this particular case the court is entitled to have before it the documents in question and it is entitled to have the independent opinion of the expert witness on those documents and on those facts—excluding, as I have said, any of the other communications which passed when the expert witness was being instructed or employed by the other side. Subject to that

60 1939 SC 472 at 479

61 1979 1 WLR 1380

> exception, it seems to me (and I would agree with the judge upon this) that the expert witness is in the same position when he is speaking as to the facts he has observed and is giving his own independent opinion on them, no matter by which side he is instructed.'
>
> 'Subject to that qualification, it seems to me that an expert witness falls into the same position as a witness of fact. The court is entitled, in order to ascertain the truth, to have the actual facts which he has observed adduced before it and to have his independent opinion on those facts. It is interesting to see that it was so held in Canada in *McDonald Construction Co Ltd v Bestway Lath & Plastering Co Ltd (1972) 27 D.L.R. (3d) 253*. In this particular case the court is entitled to have before it the documents in question and it is entitled to have the independent opinion of the expert witness on those documents and on those facts—excluding, as I have said, any of the other communications which passed when the expert witness was being instructed or employed by the other side. Subject to that exception, it seems to me (and I would agree with the judge upon this) that the expert witness is in the same position when he is speaking as to the facts he has observed and is giving his own independent opinion on them, no matter by which side he is instructed.'

In *Gary Connell Wales, William Wilson v HMA*[62] Lord Reed held:

> "The passages which I have quoted from the judgments of the Court of Appeal in the *Harmony Shipping* case appear to me to contain nothing which is inconsistent with Scots law. Viewing the matter from a Scottish perspective, I would respectfully find

[62] 2001 SCCR 633

> myself in complete agreement with the judgment of Lord Denning M.R. in that case."

On appeal, the Inner House differed from his Lordship only on the ground that the Crown had failed to establish that there was a 'good reason' in that case why they should be permitted to cite the witness who had been instructed by the defence but whom they did not intend to cite themselves.

Following from and relying upon *Harmony Shipping* and other relevant cases, it was held in Versloot Dredging BV v HDI Gerling Industrie Versicherung AG[63] that:

> "I accept, as I have already said, that the facts of these cases are different, but they seem to me to embody a wider principle. That principle is that it may be a contempt to interfere with attempts to interview a potential witness, or to prohibit the other side from getting the facts from him. Whether or not there is a contempt depends on whether the interference is improper. If it is, it does not cease to be so because the witness in question is scheduled to appear at the trial at the behest of the opposing party and may be subject to cross-examination thereat."

> "What a solicitor is not entitled to do, or indeed a party, is to order or instruct a witness or a potential witness not to attend an interview with the opposing solicitor or to tell him that he has no real choice in the matter, or to put pressure on him not to comply. Nor must he make it appear that the witness can only be interviewed if the solicitor or his principal consents."

The issue which then requires to be addressed is the proper scope of any examination in chief of the expert who it is now proposed should be called by the party which did not originally instruct them. In *Wales* the

63 [2013] EWHC 257

Inner House held[64] that "the court is likely to require to be satisfied that the evidence can be made available without any risk of disclosure of confidential information, or evidence or opinion based on such information." In *R v R*[65] Evans LJ held that:

> "The evidence which any such witness may give is limited, however, by the normal rules of legal professional privilege. These may protect communications between the witness and the defence solicitors, assuming that they were made in contemplation of legal proceedings, etc., but they do not prevent the expert from giving his or her opinion on the matters in issue."

The imperatives of a criminal trial are distinct from the requirement of a court hearing a Permanence Order application which requires the court treat the child's interests as paramount. In *Re L (A Minor) (Police Investigation)*[66] Lord Jauncey of Tullykettle held that whereas a solicitor could not without his client's consent be compelled to express an opinion on the factual or legal merits of the case, a third party who has provided a report to a client can be subpoenaed to give evidence by the other side and cannot decline to answer questions as to his factual findings and opinion thereon."

Parenting assessments

This particular species of expert report is frequently produced in permanence applications. Their utility has been questioned in appellate courts. In *City of Edinburgh Council v DG*[67] the first instance sheriff had

---

64 At 653E

65 [1994] 1 WLR 758

66 [1997] AC 16 at 25A-B

67 2019 SC 1

declined to make a Permanence Order in the belief that there should be a further parenting assessment of the father. The Lord President (Carloway) observed at paragraph 36 that:

> Quite apart from the significant delay which would then ensue, pending an assessment and a new petition process, there are two problems with this. First, the petitioners have already determined that this cannot be done by them; standing the respondent's position on the 'non-accidental' injury. Secondly, it was for the court to make that assessment based upon the evidence before it and not to delegate it to the petitioners.

In *Scottish Borders Council v Z*[68] the Sheriff Appeal Court rejected a ground of appeal against the making of a permanence order founded in the absence of a parenting assessment. The court held that "this is not fatal to the making of the order. The question for the sheriff was one of assessing the risk to Z were he to be returned to his mother. This he did on the detailed information available to him."

Excluding evidence

The powers available to the court at By Order and pre proof hearings in the Court of Session under rule 67.31 and 67.32 and in the Sheriff Court at Preliminary Hearing or Pre-Proof hearing under rules 35 and 36 Sheriff Court Adoption Rules 2009 "to make such other order as it considers appropriate for the expedition progress of the case" have been considered in *RG v Glasgow City Council.*[69] In that case, a sheriff had made extensive findings of fact following fifteen days of evidence in a Children's Referral brought by the Reporter. The local authority then began permanence proceedings and the issue in the appeal was the status

[68] 2021 Fam LR 13

[69] 2020 SC 1

of the original sheriff's findings in those later proceedings. It was agreed that the strict rules of *Res judicate* did not apply.

The division held firstly that the requirement for *res judicata* that the parties were the same in both proceedings "should not be construed too strictly". The Reporter and the local authority were both manifestations of the State whose interest were not truly different. The "essential question" in the permanence application was different from that in the children's referral and *res judicata* could not strictly apply. Nevertheless, its principles continued to "resonate".

At paragraph 32 the court went on to hold that:

> "If it is a party's intention to lead the same, or substantially the same, evidence as was presented at the ground of referral proof, and to seek only to persuade the sheriff to reach a different decision on the same evidence, the sheriff would be entitled to refuse to rehear that evidence and to find these facts established on the basis of the evidence previously heard (see now, in any event, Civil Evidence (Scotland) Act 1988 (cap 32), sec 2 ; see also Dickson, *Evidence* , p 268). In so doing he would be paying due heed to the principle behind the plea of *res judicata (supra)* that issues should not be litigated repeatedly between the same parties on substantially the same basis. A sheriff ought to take that approach if no new material is presented."

If, however, it is intended to adduce new evidence not available at the original referral, "the sheriff will have to decide whether it is of such quality and strength that it may successfully undermine the material findings of non-accidental injury made by the sheriff after the ground of referral proof."

The procedure set out in *RG* precludes a party arguing aspects of their case and its application must be strictly construed for the reason. It was a case in which the court had made considered findings on contested evidence. The position where grounds of referral are established without evidence being heard is crucially different.

The status of such concessions was considered in *M v Constanda* [70] where it was held at 354 that:

> "They are not evidence of the material facts in the statement of facts presented to the sheriff hearing the application in respect of the third child. They provide evidence to establish that the appellant has previously accepted the facts contained in the statements of facts referred to in those interlocutors."

There is a contrary indication in *City of Edinburgh Council v DG* [71] where, in respect of conceded grounds the Lord President (Carloway) observed that:

> "The supporting facts for the original ground of referral were that the child had been 'handled inappropriately and recklessly whilst in the care of his parents' and no one else had the care of the child at the relevant time. This was accepted fact and not just a real possibility."

The evidential status of conceded Grounds of Referral is therefore presently unclear and requires resolution by the Inner House given the apparent inconsistency of their decisions.

The powers of the Sheriff at common law were considered in the case of *Scottish Ministers v Stirton*[72] where it was held that "any court has the inherent power to prevent any abuse of process in the course of proceedings before it. In my opinion, that power extends to controlling

---

70 1999 SC 348

71 1999 SC 1 at Para 32

72 2009 SCLR 54

the citation of individuals as witnesses and the excusal of those who have been cited from complying with their citations."

Confidentiality

By rule 47 Sheriff Court Adoption Rule 2009:

> (1) Unless the sheriff otherwise directs, all documents lodged in process including the reports by the curator *ad litem* and reporting officer shall be available only to the sheriff, the curator *ad litem*, the reporting officer and the parties; and such documents must be treated as confidential by any persons involved in, or a party to, the proceedings and by the sheriff clerk.
>
> (2) The reporting officer and the curator *ad litem*—
>
> > (a) must treat all information obtained in the exercise of their duties as confidential; and
> >
> > (b) must not disclose any such information to any person unless disclosure of such information is necessary for the purpose of their duties.

CHAPTER FIVE

THE THRESHOLD CRITERIA

"The threshold is there to protect both the children and their parents from unjustified intervention in their lives."[73]

Permanence Order

Section 84 (5) (c) (ii) sets out the threshold which must be established before a threshold order may be made:

(i) there is no person who has the right mentioned in subsection (1)(a) of section 2 of the 1995 Act to have the child living with the person or otherwise to regulate the child's residence, or

(ii) where there is such a person, the child's residence with the person is, or is likely to be, seriously detrimental to the welfare of the child.

This sets out the "first issue of law"[74] in deciding whether to make a Permanence Order. In *KR v Stirling Council*[75] it was observed that "any court in considering whether or not to impose a permanence order must have regard to the fact that the test in subs.(5) is a threshold test, and that

---

[73] *Re B (A Child) (Care Proceedings: Appeal)* [2013] UKSC 33 per Baroness Hale of Richmond

[74] *TW v Aberdeenshire Council* 2013 138 at [12]

[75] 2016 SLT 689 at [15]

it must be satisfied before the other provisions of s.84 become relevant." Section 84 (5) (c) (ii) has two components which – "likely" and "serious detrimental" which require separate treatment which the former being considered first.

The date upon which the threshold must be established it the date upon which the court makes its evaluation.[76]

Seriously detrimental

In *KR v Stirling Council*[77] it was further observed that "mere detriment to the welfare of the child is not enough to satisfy the threshold test; serious detriment is required."

In *Dundee City Council v LT*[78] a petitioner for a Permanence Order was refused by Sheriff S G Collins QC

> "it is of course quite possible that for AT to reside with the respondent may cause him some detriment in relation to his emotional and behavioural development. It is quite possible that the respondent may be unable to provide optimum parenting in this regard. It is quite possible that AT would not get the degree of family stability and security which might be provided were he to be adopted. But none of this entitles the court to make the order which the petitioner seeks. On the whole evidence led I have not been satisfied that for AT to reside with the respondent would be likely to be seriously detrimental to his welfare."

---

76 TW v Aberdeenshire Council; City of Edinburgh Council v GD

77 At [19]

78 2015 Fam LR 145

In *West Lothian Council v B*[79] the Supreme Court approved dicta of Hedley J in *In re L (A Child) (Care: Threshold Criteria)*[80]

> "It follows inexorably from that, that society must be willing to tolerate very diverse standards of parenting, including the eccentric, the barely adequate and the inconsistent. It follows too that children will inevitably have both very different experiences of parenting and very unequal consequences flowing from it. It means that some children will experience disadvantage and harm, while others flourish in atmospheres of loving security and emotional stability. These are the consequences of our fallible humanity and it is not the provenance of the State to spare children all the consequences of defective parenting.'

The serious detriment test is a factual one which requires findings on a balance of probability. In *EV (a child)*[81] Lord Reed cited with approval two speeches given in the English case of *Re J* [82]. The first is that of Baroness Hale of Richmond in which she said that[83]:

> 'Care courts are often told that the best predictor of the future is the past. But prediction is only possible where the past facts are proved. A real possibility that something has happened in the past is not enough to predict that it will happen in the future. It may be the fact that a judge has found that there is a real possibility that something has happened. But that is not sufficient for this purpose. A finding of a real possibility that a child has suffered harm does not establish that he has."

---

79 2017 UKSC 67 at para 28

80 [2007] 1 F.L.R. 2050

81 [2017] UKSC 15

82 [2013] UKSC 9

83 At para [22]

The second was that of Lord Hope of Craighead[84] "the golden rule must surely be that a prediction of future harm has to be based on facts that have been proved on a balance of probabilities."

In determining whether particular allegations made by the applicants are proved to that requisite standard, the court must apply the words of Lord Hoffman in *Re B (Children) (Care Proceedings: Standard of Proof)*:

> 'If a legal rule requires a fact to be proved (a "fact in issue"), a judge or jury must decide whether or not it happened. There is no room for a finding that it might have happened. The law operates a binary system in which the only values are zero and one. The fact either happened or it did not. If the tribunal is left in doubt, the doubt is resolved by a rule that one party or the other carries the burden of proof. If the party who bears the burden of proof fails to discharge it, a value of zero is returned and the fact is treated as not having happened. If he does discharge it, a value of one is returned and the fact is treated as having happened.'

It is impermissible to proceed on the basis that the applicants had 'a reasonable basis for concern' as occurred at first instance in *EV*[85] or a 'real possibility' that an event occurred as in *Re B.*

Whilst in most cases the threshold will focus upon the quality of care which a parent can provide, it may be established by the perceived effect of removing the child from a settled placement away from the parental home. In *West Lothian v A & B*[86] Lord Glennie found firstly that:

> I do not find it established that M's parenting shortcomings alone would or should prevent the children being returned to

84 At para 23

85 Para {18}

86 [2016] CSOH 50

> her care. There are shortcomings, plainly, but they could be substantially overcome with time and support; and they are not such, in any event, as to lead to the conclusion that returning the children to her care would, on that account, be seriously detrimental to their welfare.[87]

However, his Lordship secondly found that:

> In my opinion there is a serious though unquantifiable risk that any attempt to rehabilitate the children, or even one of them, to her care would end in failure. That would cause enormous disruption to their lives at a very vulnerable time. Their present placements, where they are settled in and very happy, might well not be available to them. In those circumstances I am satisfied that returning the children to live with their mother is likely to be seriously detrimental to their welfare.

The latter point is also made in *Glasgow City Council, Petitioners*[88] per Lady Wise and in *East Lothian, Petitioner*[89]

In Scottish Borders Council v Z[90] the Sheriff Appeal Court held that:

> "There may very well be cases where such a move could be said to be likely to cause serious detriment to a child, without other factors being present (e.g. *East Lothian Council v LM*), but the approach of the court should always be to consider all aspects of the evidence when deciding the serious detriment test. Factors such as the length of rehabilitation, and the risk of relapse also need to be considered. At one end of the spectrum there may

---

87 Para 96

88 2019 CSOH 25

89 2019 GWD 6-75

90 2021 Fam LR 13

> well be cases where the threshold test can be passed only on the basis of serious detriment resulting from the removal from a safe secure placement and its effects. At the other end, there could be a myriad of factors in play."

A related issue arose in *Midlothian Council v CMP*[91] in which the evidence was that the mother had successfully addressed the harmful behaviour which had resulted in the children's removal from her care. The Inner House endorsed[92] the approach of the Lord Ordinary who had held:

> '[S]erious detriment would arise from failing to confirm the current settled and secure situation, which has prevailed since the child's birth, and which can safely see her through to adulthood.'
>
> 'In my opinion it cannot be concluded that there would be no serious risks in rehabilitating the child to the respondent's care. If it was tried, but failed, the serious damage to the child is obvious".

Likely

Having established in a balance of probability the facts which upon which a conclusion of serious detriment may be made, the court must then decide whether that is likely if the child lived with the relevant adult. In *Re H (a Child) In Re H. and Others (Minors) (Sexual Abuse: Standard of Proof)* [93]Lord Nichols of Birkenhead held in relation to the term in the English threshold that "the context shows that in section 31(2)(a) likely is being used in the sense of a real possibility, a possibility that cannot

91 2013 CSIH 71

92 At paragraph 24

93 [1996] AC 563 at 585

sensibly be ignored having regard to the nature and gravity of the feared harm in the particular case." This was adopted by Baroness Hale in *Re J (Children) (Care Proceedings: Threshold Criteria)*[94] which was in turn followed in *West Lothian Council v B.*[95] In *City of Edinburgh Council v DV* the Lord President, under reference to Lady Hale, held at paragraph 32 that:

> "On the proven facts, where the child is being returned to exactly the same environment in which he had suffered injury, there must be, in the absence of a material alteration in circumstances, a real possibility of present or future serious detriment"

The English authorities go somewhat further in the in *S-B (Children)* [96] the Supreme Court held that the more serious the potential harm, the lower the level of likelihood was required.

"Uncertain Perpetrators"

If the child would be returned to the care of a person who is within a pool of possible perpetrators of abuse, it is not necessary to establish that that individual was responsible. This is the effect of *Edinburgh Council v GD* in its adoption of the ratio of the English so called 'uncertain perpetrator' cases. In this case the accepted Grounds of Referral recorded that the child had been injured whilst in the joint care of his parents. The Lord President (Carloway) observed that "the sheriff's finding in fact that 'who caused' the injuries and in what circumstances 'remains unknown'

94 [2013] UKSC 9 at Para 15

95 [2017] UKSC 15

96 [2010] 1 AC 678

is accurate only to the limited extent that it is not known which of the parents was directly involved."[97] He then held that:

> "The fact that the sheriff failed to establish which parent caused the injuries is of minimal significance to the threshold issue in these circumstances. On the proven facts, where the child is being returned to exactly the same environment in which he had suffered injury, there must be, in the absence of a material alteration in circumstances, a real possibility of present or future serious detriment."

Once it has been established on a balance of probability that the child has been harmed, if not is not possible to attribute responsibility to identified individuals to the same standard, it is sufficient that the pool of potential perpetrators is comprised of persons about which there is a 'real possibility' that they caused the harm.[98] "When looking at how best to protect the child and provide for his future, the judge will have to consider the strength of that possibility as part of the overall circumstances of the case."

Authority to Adopt

Where there is an application for such authority in the petition, the court is required to consider it only after establishing that the threshold for a Permanence Order in section 84 (5) (c) (ii) has been proven. Such authority may only be part of a Permanence Order and cannot be free-standing. In *East Lothian v S* [99] an application was remitted on appeal where the sheriff had granted authority to adopt without first considering whether the threshold for a Permanence Order had been established.

---

[97] Paragraph 32

[98] *Re S-B (Children) (Care Proceedings; Standard of Proof)* [2010] 1 AC 678 at [42]

[99] 2011 Fam LR 80

However in *R v Stirling Council* [100] where the sheriff had found that residence with the mother would be "detrimental" rather than "seriously detrimental" the Inner House made its own finding of serious detriment in the facts found by the sheriff and therefore upheld the Authority to Adopt which he had granted.

The effect of section 83 (1) (c) is that authority to adopt may only be granted if the parent consents or the court dispenses with their consent. The grounds for dispensing with consent are contained in section 83 (2) and (3) of the 2007 Act namely:

> (2) Those grounds are—
>
> > (a) that the parent or guardian is dead,
> >
> > (b) that the parent or guardian cannot be found or is incapable of giving consent,
> >
> > (c) that subsection (3) or (4) applies,
> >
> > (d) that, where neither of those subsections applies, the welfare of the child otherwise requires the consent to be dispensed with.
>
> (3) This subsection applies if the parent or guardian—
>
> > (a) has parental responsibilities or parental rights in relation to the child other than those mentioned in sections 1(1)(c) and 2(1)(c) of the 1995 Act,
> >
> > (b) is, in the opinion of the court, unable satisfactorily to—

[100] 2016 SLT 69 in para [20]

(i) discharge those responsibilities, or

(ii) exercise those rights, and

(c) is likely to continue to be unable to do so.

The Relationship between the alternative tests

The effect of the wording in the subsections is that the court must first consider whether or not the 'incapacity test' has established before it may address the alternative ground that the welfare of the child requires the consent to be dispensed with. Where, however, the incapacity test is proved it is unnecessary to consider the welfare test.[101] In *Fife Council, Applicants* the Sheriff granted authority to adopt on having found the alternative grounds proven in relation to each parent. In respect of the mother he was satisfied that the 'incapacity test' established. In relation to the father he was not so satisfied but made the order because the child's welfare required it.

In *CM and CA v CH and DB*[102] the Sheriff Appeal Court held that:

> "The suggestion by the second appellant that having established the incapacity ground that the summary sheriff should not consider the welfare ground is misconceived. It is essential that a first instance judge should address all arguments made in order that their reasoning on each aspect may be reviewed if required on appeal. Section 31(4) and 31(3)(d) are alternative grounds. "[103]

---

[101] *Fife Council Applicants* [2015] CSIH 74 at {58]

Unreported

[103] See also *BH & EH v CH & SM* 2019 SAC (Civ) 7

That case contains a cautionary tale because the Sheriff Appeal Court found that the Sheriff's finding on the incapacity ground was not sustained on the findings which she had made. Her findings on the welfare ground were however held to be sufficient. If she had followed the guidance of *Fife, Applicants* and not proceeded to consider the welfare ground after establishing incapacity, the appeal is likely to have been sustained and the order recalled.

Section 83 sets out threshold criteria which must be established on a balance of probability, The court can rely on the same body of evidence as heard in support of the Permanence Order.[104]

In that fact finding exercise, article 8 ECHR considerations have no role. This was established in *S, Petitioners*[105] adopting dicta of Lord Neuberger in Re, B (A Child) (Care Proceedings: Threshold Criteria)[106]

> I consider that article 8 of the Convention … has no part to play in deciding whether the threshold is crossed, although it obviously comes very much into play when considering the issue of whether to make a care order. The threshold merely represents a hurdle which has to be crossed before the court can go on to consider whether to make a substantive order – i e an order which actually has an effect on a child and her parents (and sometimes on others). It is, of course, common ground that the court must consider any Convention rights before deciding whether to make a substantive order."
>
> [41] Applying that reasoning to a case where the issue is whether or not to dispense with parental consent to an adoption order, it would follow that art.8 has no part to play when considering whether or not the incapacity ground applies or when deciding,

---

[104] *S v Edinburgh City Council* 2013 Fam LR 2

[105] 2014 Fam LR 23

[106] 2013 1 WLR 1911

for the purposes of the welfare ground, what are the welfare requirements of an individual child.

In relation to the incapacity test, 'likely to be unable to do so' means in the foreseeable future.[107] This may be factually complex where the relevant parent has begun successfully to address the concerns which established the 'seriously detrimental' threshold at the time of the proof. In *S v City of Edinburgh Council* the Inner House dealt with that issue at paragraph 29:

> "Absent any reliable evidence (which the sheriff accepted) demonstrating a change in the pattern of behaviour which had caused the concerns in the past, it is our opinion that the sheriff was entitled to base his assessment of the future upon the substantial body of evidence relating to the present and to the past: cf. the sheriff's note at p.83 of the appeal print. That evidence was, in our view, clearly sufficient to entitle the sheriff to reach the view that the appellant was (and remained) unable satisfactorily to discharge parental responsibilities or exercise parental rights and was likely to continue to be unable to do so."

Fife Council additionally establishes that the checklist in section 14 of the Act is also engaged when determining whether to dispense with the parents' consent.[108] In *LO v N, C*[109] an adoption order was recalled by the Inner House on the ground, amongst others, that the Sheriff had failed to consider the matters set out in section 14 when deciding to dispense with the mother's consent.

---

[107] *TW v Aberdeenshire Council* [2012] SC 108 para [16]

[108] See also *East Lothian v S* 2012 CSIH

[109] 2017 CSIH 14

Welfare ground

The factors which require examination when the court is considering whether to dispense with the parents' consent to adoption on the alternative ground are relevant to each of the several parts of the Act which address welfare and are therefore considered together in the next chapter.

Subsequent Adoption Petition

The effect of a Permanence Order with Authority to Adopt on a later adoption petition was considered in the case of *AB and CD v DK.*[110] It was concerned with the position of a father without PRR who had not engaged in the proceedings relating to the POA but sought to oppose the making of an adoption order. His appeal against the making of that order was unopposed. The Sheriff Appeal Court held[111] that:

> The consent of the parents in this case has been dealt with. The respondent's consent was never required. The 2007 Act, the 2007 Rules and the cases referred to give to him limited rights. We do not consider that the respondent is entitled to seek to open up issues which, in substance, relate to the making of the POA in so far as it relates to consent. Put another way, he cannot be in a better position to oppose the making of an AO than one of the natural parents whose consent has been dispensed with. Any material which the respondent wishes to put before the court ought to relate to the interests of the child and a sheriff is entitled to scrutinise any such material robustly. (…) In making an AO the court is not limited to consideration of consent only."

110 2019 SC (SAC) 78

111 At {24}

In *East Lothian Council, Petitioners*[112] the Inner House considered the requirements for intimation of an adoption petition after a Permanence Order with Authority to Adopt had been granted. Lady Smith drew attention to the discretionary power in rule 14 (f) of the Sheriff Court Adoption Rules 2009. This empowers the sheriff to order the sheriff clerk "to intimate the application to such other person in such terms as he considers appropriate. At paragraph 28 her Ladyship observed:

> "Whilst the sheriff thus has a discretion when it comes to intimation of the adoption application, it will be incumbent on the court to consider whether or not, having regard to the whole circumstances including the parents' Convention rights there requires to be such intimation (Ghaidan v Godin-Mendoza, per Lord Rodger of Earlsferry at [2004] 2 A.C., pp.594—595, paras 106—107). Since the procedure involves the court being notified of any permanence order, if that order includes provision for contact between the child and a member of his natural family, we would expect the court to intimate the adoption application to any such family member, bearing in mind the art.8 rights involved."

Such a person may therefore seek to preserve any extant contract provisions in a subsequent adoption order. The nature of any other "limited rights" referred to in *AB and CD v DK* remains unexplored.

[112] 2012 Fam LR 7

CHAPTER SIX

WELFARE

In addition to the welfare ground for dispensing with consent to making of an order granting authority to adopt applying section 83 (2) (d) of the 2007 Act, welfare arises in numerous other provisions of the Act. The court is required to consider whether it is better for the child that the order is made than if it should not be made in relation to permanence orders[113] and granting authority to adopt[114]. It is required to "regard the need to safeguard and promote the welfare of the child throughout childhood as the paramount consideration" when deciding whether to make a permanence order.[115] When considering an application for Authority to Adopt, the court is directed to section 14 (3) of the Act which requires it to "regard the need to safeguard and promote the welfare of the child throughout the child's life as the paramount consideration."

"Welfare" is intimately related to the rights under Article 8 of the ECHR which are held by all the human parties to permanence proceedings. The case of *Strand Lobben v Norway*[116] consolidates the existing jurisprudence of the ECrtHR on the Article 8 considerations in public law children's cases. In paragraphs 202 and 203 they summarise the foundation principles of Article 8:

> 202. The first paragraph of art.8 of the Convention guarantees to everyone the right to respect for his or her family life. As is

[113] Section 84 (3) 2007 Act

[114] Section 83 91) (d) 2007 Act

[115] Section 84 (4) 2007 Act

[116] (2020) 70 EHRR 14

> well established in the Court's case-law, the mutual enjoyment by parent and child of each other's company constitutes a fundamental element of family life, and domestic measures hindering such enjoyment amount to an interference with the right protected by this provision. Any such interference constitutes a violation of this article unless it is "in accordance with the law", pursues an aim or aims that is or are legitimate under its second paragraph and can be regarded as "necessary in a democratic society".
>
> 203. In determining whether the latter condition was fulfilled, the Court will consider whether, in the light of the case as a whole, the reasons adduced to justify that measure were relevant and sufficient for the purposes of para.2 of art.8 . The notion of necessity further implies that the interference corresponds to a pressing social need and, in particular, that it is proportionate to the legitimate aim pursued, regard being had to the fair balance which has to be struck between the relevant competing interests.
>
> (...)
>
> 206 In instances where the respective interests of a child and those of the parents come into conflict, art.8 requires that the domestic authorities should strike a fair balance between those interests and that, in the balancing process, particular importance should be attached to the best interests of the child which, depending on their nature and seriousness, may override those of the parents."

The concepts of necessity and proportionality are also emphasised in the domestic authorities starting with an examination of the corresponding welfare provision relating to direct adoption petition was considered by the Supreme Court in *S v L*[117] where it was held at paragraph 34 that:

> "(...) legislation authorising the severing of family ties between parents and their children will not readily be construed as setting anything less than a test of necessity. Section 31(3)(d) , in stipulating that the welfare of the child must 'require' that parental consent be dispensed with, is consistent with such a test. There must, in other words, be an overriding requirement that the adoption proceed for the sake of the child's welfare, which remains the paramount consideration. The court must be satisfied that the interference with the rights of the parents is proportionate: in other words, that nothing less than adoption will suffice. If the child's welfare can be equally well secured by a less drastic intervention, then it cannot be said that the child's welfare 'requires' that consent to adoption should be dispensed with."

This was followed in the English care of *Re B (a Child) (Care Proceedings: Appeal)*[118] which contained a passage which is frequently cited in argument and judgements in Scottish Courts:

> "Nevertheless, it is quite clear that the test for severing the relationship between parent and child is very strict: only in exceptional circumstances and where motivated by overriding requirements pertaining to the child's welfare, in short, where nothing else will do. In many cases, and particularly where the feared harm has not yet materialised and may never do so, it will be necessary to explore and attempt alternative solutions."

---

[117] 2012 UKSC 30

[118] [2013] UKSC 33

Some refinement of that approach is evident in the approach of Sir Andrew MacFarlane P in the case of *Re W (a child)*[119] commenting on 'nothing else will do':

> "The phrase is meaningless, and potentially dangerous, if it is applied as some freestanding, shortcut test divorced from, or even in place of, an overall evaluation of the child's welfare. Used properly, as Baroness Hale explained, the phrase "nothing else will do" is no more, nor no less, than a useful distillation of the proportionality and necessity test as embodied in the ECHR and reflected in the need to afford paramount consideration to the welfare of the child throughout her lifetime (ACA 2002 s 1). The phrase "nothing else will do" is not some sort of hyperlink providing a direct route to the outcome of a case so as to bypass the need to undertake a full, comprehensive welfare evaluation of all of the relevant pros and cons."

The Inner House has revisited the necessity and proportionality tests in permanence cases twice. In *North Lanarkshire Council v KR*[120] it was held that once the threshold was met the court had to consider those issues in the context of a child who would not be returning to her parent's care:

> "Once the sheriff has decided that the threshold tests in ss. 84(5) and (83)(2) have been met, it is clearly the case that a child will not be returned in the near future to live with the person who has parental rights with regard to the child. That being so, the court requires to consider what are the various options available for the care of the child. Having identified the various options, the court then requires to carry out an assessment of the proportionality of each of these options. This will involve an assessment of the practicality of each option, and the possible benefits and disbenefits to the child's welfare of each option.

[119] [2016] EWCA 793

[120] [2018] CSIH 59 at para 64

> This is an exercise which is looking to the future, but which is informed to an important extent by findings in fact relating to past and present facts and circumstances, because future assessments cannot be based merely on hope or speculation, but must be grounded in sufficient findings-in-fact of what has happened or is now happening."

In that case the sheriff had declined to make a permanence order with authority to adopt which had been sought by the petitioner local authority. He found that "there was however room for further intervention before a decision on permanence was taken and that remains [121]the case. It has therefore not been established that the making of a permanence order with or without authority to adopt is necessary." The Inner House found that the absence of evidence of available interventions and the sheriff's failure to engage in an evaluation of the options for the child's care resulted in the appeal being allowed and the order sought being granted.

The English case of *Re E (a Child)* [122] establishes that the failure of the local authority to provide support to the parent is a relevant factor in determining the proportionality of any outcome to the application for an order.

In *City of Edinburgh v GD*[123] the Lord President held at paragraph 35 that:

> "In the new equation, of whether or not it would be better to grant the Permanence Order and authority to adopt, there is a legal assumption, deriving especially from Article 8 of the European Convention on Human Rights (see also at common law: *Sanderson v McManus 1997 SC (HL) 55*), that a child is

[122] [2013] EWCA 1592

[123] [2018] CSIH 52

> best brought up in family by and with his parents, or at least one of them, and that an order which alters that situation should only be made when it is "necessary" as a last resort ("nothing else will do"). The only way in which that principle can be reconciled with the potentially conflicting consideration, that the welfare of the child is paramount, is to proceed on the basis that, where a child's welfare is better protected by a Permanence Order, that order must be deemed necessary in the interests of that child.

Alternative Orders

In *Fife Council, Applicants*[124] at paragraph 63 Lord Bracadale drew the following propositions from the English case of *Re B-S (Children) (Adoption: Leave to Oppose)*[125]

> "First, there was a requirement for proper evidence which must address all the options which were realistically possible and must contain an analysis of the arguments for and against each option. Secondly, there must be an adequately reasoned judgment."

Otherwise, the English authorities which emphasise the need to consider other reasonable alternatives in order to determine whether the order south is proportionate require to be treated with caution in the Scottish context. In considering the reasonable options an English judge has a blank canvas in which they can make a range of orders which place the child outwith local authority care.

In Scotland, most children about whom a court is considering whether to make a permanence order will already be the subject of a Compulsory Supervision Order. The court can only revoke the CSO under section 89 of the 2007 Act if it makes a Permanence Order and not if it declines to

124 2016 SC 169

125 [2014] 1 WLR 563

do so. The CSO remains in place and the case of *Aitken v Aitken* 1978 SC 297 makes clear that the exercise of any parental rights or responsibilities is subject to the conditions attached to the CSO. This did not inhibit Sheriff Paul Reid in *C v J*[126] from making a Residence Order where the child remained within the Children's Hearing system. However, this was a kinship care placement supported by the local authority who would then revert to the Children's Hearing to consider their future role.

In *LO v N, C*[127] the Inner House, in recalling an adoption order made at first instance held that:

> We consider that s.11 (1) is framed in terms sufficiently broad to give the court power in adoption proceedings to make such an order under s.11 of the 1995 Act or such an order could be made in separate proceedings raised for that purpose. We are unpersuaded that the sheriff made any reasoned assessment of whether there were any alternatives, short of adoption, which would secure the welfare of E in all the circumstances of this case

In *AV & SV v AJF & IDF*[128] Lady Wise observed obiter that it would be competent to make a section 11 order in adoption proceedings. *BH & EH v CH and SM*[129] the Sheriff Appeal Court is to like effect. All of these cases are direct adoption petitions and in none of them was a section 11 order made. In each the candidate for a section 11 order was the prospective adopters, not a third party.

---

[126] 2022 GWD 33-489

[127] 2017 Fam LR 44 at 29

[128] 2017 Fam LR 110

[129] 2019 Fam LR 47

There is a first instance decision of Sheriff Daniel Kelly QC[130] in which he made s 11 orders in favour of the petitioner instead of the adoption order for which she applied relying on the *ex proprio muto* powers in section 11 (3) (b) and having concluded that an adoption order was neither necessary nor proportionate.

In *BH* the Sheriff Appeal Court held that, where a section 11 order is made within an adoption petition, any application to vary it should be by fresh proceedings begun by initial writ, rather than a minute within the adoption petition.

The possibility of making a section 11 order as an alternative to a Permanence Order with or without Authority to Adopt has not been fully developed in the authorities. There is no principled reason why the logic which underpins the decisions considered above should not apply to permanence as to adoption. Section 11 (1) and (3) (b) apply equally to permanence and adoption proceedings.

Kinship care

The obvious context in which it might be appropriate to make a section 11 order as an alternative to a Permanence Order is in a kinship care arrangement. In *CEC v EAH*[131] Sheriff Welsh QC declined to make a Permanence Order with Authority to Adopt because he considered that the maternal aunt had not been adequately considered for kinship care.

'Kinship carer' is defined in regulation 10 Looked After Children (Scotland) Regulations 2009 as:

(a) a person who is related to the child; or

[130] X v Y 2015 Fam LR 41

[131] 2018 GWD 18-234

(b) a person who is known to the child and with whom the child has a pre-existing relationship.

Kinship care arises in three distinct contexts in the permanence process. Firstly, it may be an alternative to a permanence application. Secondly, it may be a proposed placement within a Permanence Order. Finally, it may be an alternative order made by the court in place of the permanence order sought by the petitioners.

An example of the first approach is in the case of *J v C* in which the local authority determined that permanence was in the child's best interests and supported a relative to apply for a Residence Order.

Section 71 Children and Young People (Scotland) Act 2014 requires a local authority to provide support to potential kinship carers and children who might be suitable for such a placement.

Before placing the child with a Kinship Carer the local authority must have completed an assessment as required by Regulation 10 of the Looked After Children (Scotland) Regulations 2009. They must be satisfied under regulation 11 that placement is in the best interests of the child and does not conflict with the terms of a Compulsory Supervision Order. The placement must be supported by a written agreement between the carer and the local authority.

The local authority may then support the kinship carer to apply for a 'Kinship Care Order' as defined in section 72 of the Act Of 2014 namely:

(a) an order under section 11(1) of the 1995 Act which gives to a qualifying person the right mentioned in section 2(1)(a) of that Act in relation to a child,

(b) a residence order which has the effect that a child is to live with, or live predominantly with, a qualifying person, or

(c) an order under section 11(1) of the 1995 Act appointing a qualifying person as a guardian of a child.

The second scenario is where the intended placement under a Permanence Order is with a kinship carer. An avowed purpose of the Permanence Order regime was that "foster career should be able to use the order to "claim" the child by acquiring some parental rights and responsibilities".[132] Thus, an ancillary order under section 82 (1) (b) can vest in a foster or kinship carer all of the parental responsibilities and parental rights contained in ss 1 and 2, Children (Scotland) Act 1995

Finally, the prospective family carer who does not have the support of the local authority which is a prerequisite of the two scenarios considered above may seek to participate in the permanence proceedings as "a person who claims to have an interest" under rule 67.30 (b) (i) RCS or rule 33 Sheriff Court Adoption Rules 2009. This would enable them to seek to persuade the court to exercise its powers under section 11 (1) and (3) by making a Residence Order in their favour. This was unsuccessfully attempted in *JA, TA, JC v Mr & Mrs AC*

A relative who obtained a section 11 order within permanence proceedings against the opposition of the local authority would not be a kinship carer approved under Part V of the Looked After Children (Scotland) Regulations 2009 and therefore not entitled the support available within a Kinship Care Agreement made in Schedule 5 to those Regulations.

[132] *Adoption: Better Choices for Our Children. Report of Phase II* para 5.12

CHAPTER SEVEN

CONTACT

Orders for contact made in permanence proceedings as especially case sensitive and principle is difficult to identify from the scant case law on the point. There are however recognisable differences in the contexts in which such orders are considered.

The public law setting gives rise to considerations which are absent in private law applications under section 11 Children (Scotland) Act 1995. The leading authority outlining the correct approach to such applications is the case of *J v M*[133] where the Inner House held at paragraphs 11 and 12 that:

> (1) in terms of s.11(7)(a) of the 1995 Act, the judge must treat the welfare of the child as the paramount consideration. The issue is — what is best for the child? (…) The court must have regard to a number of specified matters, including the need to protect the child from any abuse (defined as including any conduct likely to cause distress), and the need for co-operation between the parents: s.11(7A–E) .
>
> (2) Before refusing an application for parental contact, a careful balancing exercise must be carried out with a view to identifying whether there are weighty factors which make such a serious step necessary and justified in the paramount interests of the child (sometimes referred to as "exceptional circumstances"). (…) This approach is reflective of the

[133] 2016 SC 835

general background of it almost always being conducive to the welfare of a child that parental contact is maintained.

(…)

12 Having reviewed the opinion of the court in M v K , we are not persuaded that the court had any intention to go beyond the proposition that, since in general it is strongly in the interests of a child to maintain a relationship with both parents, before a contrary position is taken, the court must, after carefully weighing all the relevant circumstances, identify factors which justify such a serious step and demonstrate that it is conducive to the welfare of the child. (…)

The 'relevant circumstances' are case specific and differ according to the nature of the substantive order which the court is considering making.

Permanence Order

A Permanence Order without Authority to Adopt may contain ancillary orders extinguishing the right of parents to exercise parental responsibilities and parental rights. They do not thereby cease to be the child's parents. This is distinct from the plan envisaged by granting Authority to Adopt.

Contact within a Permanence Order without Authority to Adopt was considered in the Sheriff Appeal Court in the case of *East Lothian v L*[134]. The court recognised that a Permanence Order differed from an adoption order but that measures for contact in either were determined by refence

[134] 2023 SLT (SAC) 1

to the child's best interests.[135] The Sheriff in the court below had been alter to the differences between the two types of order and had not started from a presumption against contact. He had adopted the correct approach in a permanence case when he stated:

> "Against this background, I agree with the petitioner's position that the opportunity for [ZL] to benefit from the new found stability and security provided by the permanence order must be prioritised over birth family contact. While that is not something that ZL's family agree with, they must understand that it is not their interests that the court is considering – the court is focused on [ZL] and his best interests."
>
> In these words the sheriff made it clear that his decision to reduce the level of contact between ZL and his birth family was based on these considerations and therefore that the decision was based upon the welfare principle. Accordingly he correctly applied the terms of section 84(4) of the 2007 Act ."

It is not difficult to understand why an appeal was taken in this case. Whilst stating that Permanence and Adoption Orders were different, the Sheriff cited an adoption case at some length. The Sheriff Appeal Court however observed that " (…) adoption is a very different situation from a permanence order because the subject of adoption becomes in law the child of the adopters exclusively, by virtue of ss. 40(1) –(4)) of the Adoption and Children (Scotland) Act 2007 . The birth parents' parental rights and responsibilities relating to the child are extinguished on adoption (*ibid* ss. 35(2)).

---

135 Under reference to *East Lothian Council, Petitioners* [2012] CSIH 3, 2012 Fam. L.R. 7

Authority to Adopt

When the court grants authority to adopt it is setting in train a process in which the birth parents will cease to be the legal parents of the child and that status is comprehensively transferred to the adopters as described above. It is in that context that future arrangements for contact fall to be considered.

The law relating to post adoption contact is presently unclear and ripe for authoritative consideration. The present authorities place different emphasise on the significance of the wishes of the prospective adopters, which may or may not be known at the time the Authority to Adopt is considered.

In *AB, CD v LM*[136] Appeal Sheriff Andrew Cubie, sitting alone, obiter approved a first instance decision of Sheriff (as she then was) Aisha Anwar in an unrelated case called *Mr and Mrs P v LD*[137] in which her Ladyship set forth a check-list of factors to consider:

> (a) the nature of the child's bond with, and attachment to, the members of the birth family seeking contact; (b) the age and if appropriate, the views, of the child; (c) the level and nature of the contact currently enjoyed by the birth family, if any; (d) the benefit derived by the child from such contact, if any; (e) the risks to which the child may be exposed during such contact, if any; (f) the ability, or otherwise, of the birth family to commit to contact and to heed the advice of professionals in relation to how to manage such contact; (g) the ability, or otherwise of the birth family to accept the terms of the adoption order, to be fully supportive of it, and to refrain from undermining the adoption

---

136 2019 Fam LR 60

137 2016 SC 56

process or engaging in future litigation; and (h) the views of the adoptive parents to such contact."

This may be the future but it is apparent conflict with the authorities from the senior courts. The starting point is *B v C*[138] in which the Inner House held firstly that:

> "The guiding principle is that adoption provides complete security to the child by making the child part of the adopting parents' family. Conditions expressed in favour of third parties, which might make it necessary for the court to become involved in the making of further orders with a view to the child's welfare, will not be appropriate except in the very rare cases where the child's welfare might be prejudiced if a condition to that effect were not to be made."

Secondly that:

> "Although separate legislation relating to adoption has now been enacted for Scotland and for England and Wales, many of the statutory provisions contained in these enactments are the same. We consider that it would be undesirable for provisions which have been enacted in the same terms both north and south of the border to receive a different construction in Scotland from that which is given to them in England and Wales. Accordingly, it is appropriate that the Scottish courts should continue to look for guidance to English authority where this is available, so long as this is not in conflict with the Scottish authorities."

England and Wales is of course a much larger jurisdiction and issues frequently arise there before they do in Scotland. The issue of post adoption contact was addressed by the Court of Appeal in *Re B (A*

---

[138] 1996 SLT 1370

Child)[139] in a judgement given by Sir Andrew MacFarlane P. At paragraph 59.

> "The law remains, as I have stated it, namely that it will only be in an extremely unusual case that a court will make an order stipulating contact arrangement to which the adopters do not agree."

The caveat is contained in the paragraphs which follow:

> "(...) it must be a given that any social worker, children's guardian or expert who is required to advise the court on the issue of contact, will ensure that they are fully aware of any current research and its potential impact upon the welfare issues in each particular case. Equally, it is already a requirement that courts should give adequate and clear reasons for any orders that are made following contested proceedings.
>
> 61. Post-adoption contact is an important issue which should be given full consideration in every case."

So any change in approach which moves towards greater direct contact would take place in the stages before the adoption application is made.

Caution must be exercised when considering the relevance of academic research which is said to promote the benefits of post adoption contact. This inevitably analyses cases where contact has been ordered under existing legal principles. It therefore does little more that confirm the suitability of those principles and cannot be the basis for widening the circumstances in which post adoptive contact occurs.

---

[139] [2019] Fam 389

Ultimately, if contact is deemed to be so important to the child's welfare and the adopters are resolutely opposed to it, this raises questions as to their suitability to be the child's parents.

It is almost invariable that where there is no direct contact, bilateral indirect contact by letters and cards is ordered but typically infrequently. However, in AB, CD v LM *(ibid)* an appeal against the refusal of the Sheriff to provide for indirect contact in an adoption case was refused.

Previously, orders for the exchange of photographs were not unknown. For several years now this practice has fallen into disfavour because of cases in which the parents put the photographs on social media claiming that their child had been abducted and seeking information about their whereabouts. Sometimes orders are made which permit controlled viewing of photographs which are not available for retention. It is important to recognise that what may appear a kindness to a disappointed birth parent may in practice cause greater distress in the future.

CHAPTER EIGHT

EXPENSES

Rule 67 RSC provides that "In a cause to which this Chapter applies, the court may make such order as to expenses, including the expenses of a reporting officer, a curator ad litem, or any other person who attended a hearing, as it thinks fit." Rule 2 Sheriff Court Adoption Rules 200 is in identical terms.

The discretion so conferred is subject to principles set out in caselaw and the requirement of fairness where typically all parties except on are legally aided and therefore immune to any effective expenses order. There are, of course, rigid principles circumscribing the exercise of judicial discretion in other contexts, for example expenses follow success and expenses are rare in children's cases.

In the contact of permanence cases in *Perth and Kinross Council Petitioners*[140] it was held per Lord Brailsford that:

> "The question therefore arises, what would constitute an appropriate case in which an award of expenses should be made? Whilst I have little doubt that it would be impossible, and certainly of no practical value, to attempt to define all the circumstances where an award of expenses might be justified in a permanence petition, it does appear that some broad conclusions could be drawn. In that regard, I would observe that the care proceedings at issue in the Supreme Court English cases put before me provide useful analogies. The categories identified in these cases were where the conduct of the party, in particular a local authority, could be characterised as reprehensible or

[140] [2018] SLT 275 at paragraph 12

> where it might be said a party took an unreasonable stance in the conduct of the proceedings. I would consider that similar categories could usefully be applied in the context of permanence applications in Scotland."

The Supreme Court cases to which his Lordship refers set a high hurdle for any claim for expenses in permanence cases. The starting point is the decision of Wilson J (as he then was) in *Sutton London Borough Council v Davis (No 2)* 1 WLR 1317 at 1319 E:

> "Thus, even when a local authority's application for a care order is dismissed, it is unusual to order them to pay the costs of the other parties. But the proposition is not applied where, for example, the conduct of a party has been reprehensible or the party's stance has been beyond the band of what is reasonable: *Havering London Borough Council v. S. [1986] 1 F.L.R. 489* and *Gojkovic v. Gojkovic [1992] Fam. 40* , 60C–D."

This test was endorsed by the Supreme Court in *Re T (Children) (Care Proceedings: Costs)* [2012] 2281 at paragraph 44 per Baroness Hale of Richmond:

> "For these reasons we have concluded that the general practice of not awarding costs against a party, including a local authority, in the absence of reprehensible behaviour or an unreasonable stance, is one that accords with the ends of justice (…)"

The next consideration by the Supreme Court is in the case of *Re S (A Child) (Access to Justice Foundation intervening)* [2105] 1 WLR 1631 at paragraph 26 per Baroness Hale of Richmond:

> "All the reasons which make it inappropriate as a general rule to make costs orders in children's cases apply with equal force in care proceedings between parents and local authorities as they do in private law proceedings between parents or other family members. They lead to the conclusion that costs orders should

> only be made in unusual circumstances. Two of them were identified by Wilson J in Sutton London Borough Council v Davis (No 2) : “where, for example, the conduct of a party has been reprehensible or the party's stance has been beyond the band of what is reasonable: *Havering London Borough Council v S [1986] 1 FLR 489* and *Gojkovic v Gojkovic [1992] Fam 40* , 60C-D” (p 1319). Those were also the two circumstances identified in In re T, at para 44.”

Her Ladyship then refers at paragraph 35 to a case in which a costs order was made:

> “It is not a case like A and S (Children) v Lancashire County Council (Costs) (No 2) [2013] EWHC 851 (Fam), [2013] 2 FLR 122, where the local authority's conduct towards the children over many years was “blatantly unlawful and unreasonable ... and led inexorably to substantial litigation”

That appears to be the only such reported case and the facts are exceptional.

In paragraph 33 her Ladyship observed obiter:

> “If the best outcome for the child is to be brought up by her own family, there may be cases where real hardship would be caused if the family had to bear their own costs of achieving that outcome. In other words, the welfare of the child would be put at risk if the family had to bear its own costs. In those circumstances, just as it may be appropriate to order a richer parent who has behaved reasonably in the litigation to pay the costs of the poorer parent with whom the child is to live, it may also be appropriate to order the local authority to pay the costs of the parent with whom the child is to live, if otherwise the child's welfare would be put at risk.”

CHAPTER NINE

APPEALS

What may be appealed

Section 110 Courts Reform (Scotland) Act 2014 provides that:

(1) An appeal may be taken to the Sheriff Appeal Court, without the need for permission, against—

(a) a decision of a sheriff constituting final judgment in civil proceedings

A Permanence Order, with or without Authority to Adopt is a final judgment in civil proceedings. Furthermore appeals may be taken without permission against:

(b) any decision of a sheriff in civil proceedings—

(i) granting, refusing or recalling an interdict, whether interim or final,

(ii) granting interim decree for payment of money other than a decree for expenses,

(iii) making an order ad factum praestandum,

(iv) sisting an action,

(v) allowing, refusing or limiting the mode of proof, or

(vi) refusing a reponing note.

(1) An appeal may be taken to the Sheriff Appeal Court against any other decision of a sheriff in civil proceedings if the sheriff, on the sheriff's own initiative or on the application of any party to the proceedings, grants permission for the appeal.

In *Highland Council, Petitioner*[141] the Sheriff Appeal Court accepted that the Sheriff Court Adoption Rules did not permit a party to seek to be reponed after a Permanence Order had been made in their absence but that it was competent for them to appeal to that court without the requirement of permission. The appeal was, however, refused because there was no error by the Sheriff given the appellant's multiple failures to engage in the proceedings and the merits of the application.

It was held in *D v M*[142] that a failure to obtain permission to appeal where it is required renders the appeal incompetent. Permission must be sought in the first instance from the sheriff who made the order.

Reclaiming motions in the Court of Session are governed by Chapter 38 RCS. The number of circumstances in which reclaiming is competent without leave are more numerous than in the corresponding Sheriff Court rule. It is sufficient for present purposes that leave is not required to reclaim an interlocutor which deals with the whole merits of the cause.[143] This plainly includes Permanence Orders with or without Authority to Adopt.

---

[141] 2022 SC (SAC) 45

[142] [2020] SAC (Civ) 25

[143] Rule 38.2 RCS

It has been held, in the case of *Burns v Waddell & Sons,*[144] that an order is final only if it fully deals with expenses. This may appear a pedantic point in cases where expenses orders are exceptional.

The time for appeal in the Court of Session is defined in rule 38.2 RCS as "21 days from the date on which the interlocutor was pronounced". In the Sheriff Court rule 6.3 Sheriff Appeal Court Rules 2015 provides that "an appeal must be made within 28 days after the date on which the decision appealed against was given."

The requirements of the rules apply equally to party litigants as to those with the benefit of representation. This was decided by the Inner House in *AW, Applicant*[145] following the Supreme Court decision in *Barton v Wright Hassall LLP.*[146]

Leave to appeal after the time limit has expired under may be sought under rule 38.10 RCS or rule 6.4 Sheriff Appeal Court Rules. Reliance is then placed on rule 2.1 which permits relief from failure to comply with the rules if that was die to "mistake, oversight or other excusable cause."

The marking of a reclaiming motion or appeal has two immediate effects. Firstly, it suspends the operation of the decree.[147] Secondly, the effect of rule 38.6 RCS is that it open for review all previous interlocutors of the Lord Ordinary not only for the party reclaiming but also the other parties.

---

144 (1897) 24 R 325; *Palambo v James Jack (Hyndford) Ltd* 1977 SLT (Sh Ct) 95

145 2018 Fam LR 60

146 [2018] 1 WLR 1119

147 *Mulhern v The Scottish Police Services Authority* 2009 SLT 353

A motion for urgent disposal under Rule 38.11 RCS or rules 7.4 and 7.5 Sheriff Appeals Court Rules is typically made in children's cases if any party enrols a motion seeking such an order.

Appeals on factual findings

The Appellate Court has not had the advantage of hearing the evidence of witnesses and is not engaged in a re-examination of the first instance judge's evaluation of their evidence. In *Thomas v Thomas*[148] the House of Lord held that "where a question of fact has been tried by a Judge without a jury, and there is no question of misdirection of himself by the Judge, an appellate Court which is disposed to come to a different conclusion on the printed evidence should not do so unless it is satisfied that any advantage enjoyed by the trial Judge by reason of having seen and heard the witnesses could not be sufficient to explain or justify the trial Judge's conclusion."

The circumstances in which the appellate court engages with the factual evidence are outlined by the Inner House in *W v Greater Glasgow Health Board*[149]

> For example, the trial judge may have considered the wrong question, or may have taken account of manifestly irrelevant considerations, or may have ignored evidence that was manifestly relevant. In all these cases we consider that an appellate court may properly interfere with the findings of primary fact made by the trial judge. It can, indeed, be said that the application of the "no reasonable judge" test is an example of an error of law affecting the findings of primary fact.

[148] 1947 SC (HL) 45 at 59

[149] 2017 CSIH 58 at [52]

Appeals based on discretion

It is well established that the ambit of review by an appellate court in children's cases is restricted. In *A v B and C*[150] it was held that:

> "Adoption cases depend so much on general impression rather than the ascertainment of particular facts that, when the judge at first instance has seen the parties, an appeal court must be slow to reverse his decision unless he has misdirected himself as to the law or has otherwise clearly gone wrong." (per Lord Reid)
>
> "I should be reluctant to disturb a decision reached without error of law upon a matter which must depend to a large extent upon the impression formed by the trial judge as to the character of the mother and other witnesses. I prefer not to rely upon my own judgment but to say that there was ample evidence upon which the judge could reach his conclusion." (per Lord Simon of Glaisdale adopting dicta of Lord Guest in *Re W (An Infant)*[151]

In the English case of *G v G (Custody Appeal)*[152] the House of Lords explained the reasoning upon which this approach is founded and that it applies wherever a court is exercising a discretion. Lord Bridge adopted at 652F a passage from the judgment of Asquith LJ in a case called *Bellenden (formerly Satterthwaite) v. Satterthwaite* [153]:

> "We are here concerned with a judicial discretion, and it is of the essence of such a discretion that on the same evidence two different minds might reach widely different decisions without either being appealable. It is only where the decision exceeds the

[150] 1971 SC (HL) 129 per Lord Reid at 141

[151] [1971] AC 682

[152] [1987] 1 WLR

[153] [1948] 1 All E.R. 343

> generous ambit within which reasonable disagreement is possible, and is, in fact, plainly wrong, that an appellate body is entitled to interfere."

In Scotland this approach to the proper ambit of appellate jurisdiction has been evident across the range of children's cases. It has also been applied to private law cases in *Osborne v Matthan (No 3)*[154] where it was held that "in a case like the present where the sheriff has seen and heard the witnesses, it would be unusual for an appeal court to interfere with the sheriff's judgment on the issue of custody."[155] In *Britton v Central Regional Council*[156] the Inner House observed that:

> "In presenting his submission in support of the reclaiming motion counsel for the reclaimer recognised at the outset that this appellate court may not interfere with the decision of the Lord Ordinary unless it is satisfied either that he exercised his discretion upon a wrong principle or that, his decision being so plainly wrong, he must have exercised his discretion wrongly. There is ample authority for that proposition, and we simply refer to the most recent discussion of the matter in the speech of Lord Fraser of Tullybelton in *G. v. G. (Minors: Custody Appeal) [1985] 1 W.L.R. 647.*"

In Permanence cases with authority to adopt it has been followed in *W v Aberdeenshire Council (ibid),* In a Permanence case without Authority to Adopt it was applied in *Dundee City Council, Appellants.*[157]

---

[154] 1998 SC 682 at 689

[155] Also *McGraddie v McGraddie* 2013 SLT 1212

[156] 1986 SLT 207

[157]2016 Fam LR 128

The appealed judgment

The quest to demonstrate that the sheriff or judge in the court below was "plainly wrong" involves an analysis of their judgment. The requirements of a judgment were considered in the case of Henderson v Foxworth Investments Ltd[158] in *AB, CD v LM*[159] the Appellant sought to rely on a sentence in the Supreme Court judgment in *Henderson* which emphasised the fundamentals of a judgment. At paragraph 67 it was held that "an appellate court will interfere with the findings of fact made by a trial judge only if it is satisfied that his decision cannot reasonably be explained or justified."

In *AB, CD v LM* the Sheriff Appeal Court refusing the appeal held that *Henderson* "does not impose an obligation on the sheriff to explain each and every possible outcome or each and every advantage or disadvantage of a possible outcome."[160] They reiterated what had been said in in which the held at para 6:

> '[6] In cases such as this the sheriff requires to produce the written judgment within a very tight timescale. There may be numerous findings in fact. Often such facts are contained in a joint minute of the parties, but the sheriff still requires to consider with care each proposed finding to ensure that it is accurate, correctly expressed and supported by evidence. He or she then has to set out the evidence of the witnesses in some detail, comment upon it and reach a reasoned conclusion. That task is made more difficult when care has to be taken not to make an unintentional error in expression which can in certain circumstances lead to the impression, which might be erroneous, that the sheriff has failed to apply the Act in the required

[158] [2014] UKSC 41, [2014] 1 W.L.R. 2600, [2014] 7 WLUK 43

[159] 2019 Fam LR 60

[160] At paragraph

manner. A judgment produced in such circumstances should not be subjected to the detailed scrutiny of a conveyancing document. That point was made in the *dicta* of Lord Hoffmann in an English case on financial provision on divorce (*Piglowska v Piglowski,* at p.1372) in which he repeated what he had said in an earlier case:

> "...specific findings in fact, even by the most meticulous judge, are inherently an incomplete statement of the impression which was made on him by the primary evidence. His expressed findings are always surrounded by a penumbra of imprecision as to emphasis, relative weight, minor qualification and nuance ... of which time and language do not permit exact expression, but which may play an important part in the judge's overall evaluation.

Orders on Appeal

The primary orders at the conclusion of an appeal are either dismissal and adherence to the interlocutor of the court below or alternatives sustaining of the appeal and recall of the interlocutor of the court below.

Where it has been established that there was error in the court of first instance, the appellate court has a range of options. These are particularly apposite in children's cases where remit for rehearing may conflict with the injunction against delay. The court may simply allow the appeal and recall the order as in *LO v N, C* (ibid). It may remit the case to the Sheriff to rectify their judgement.[161] It may call for further evidence and substitute its own order as in *North Lanarkshire v KR* (ibid) where a further curator report was commissioned. It may substitute its own

[161] *Ab and CB v X's Curator* 1963 SC 124.

discretion in the facts found by the Sheriff as the Sheriff Principal had in *L v Central RC.*[162]

Appeals from the Sheriff Appeal Court to the Court of Session

Section 113 (1) Courts Reform (Scotland) Act 2014 provides that an appeal to the Court of Session requires the permission of either the Sheriff Appeal Court, or if that has been refused, the Court of Session. Such section 113 (2) requires that permission may only be given if the appeal would raise an important point of principle or practice, or there is some other compelling reason for the Court of Session to hear the appeal.

In *Politakis v Spencely*[163] the Inner House considered the meaning of section 113 (2). They held firstly that "raising an important point of principle or practice is a reference to one which has not yet been established. It does not include a question of whether an established principle or practice has been correctly applied." Secondly, that when considering whether some other compelling reason existed, it was important to emphasise the 'truly exceptional nature of the jurisdiction' in relation to second appeals. 'Compelling' is a 'very strong word', albeit that the test is there to enable the court to deal with the case justly. A good starting point is a consideration of the prospects of success".

[162] 1990 SLT 818.

[163] 2018 SC 184

APPENDIX ONE

ADOPTION AND CHILDREN (SCOTLAND) ACT 2007

14 Considerations applying to the exercise of powers

(1) Subsections (2) to (4) apply where a court or adoption agency is coming to a decision relating to the adoption of a child.

(2) The court or adoption agency must have regard to all the circumstances of the case.

(3) The court or adoption agency is to regard the need to safeguard and promote the welfare of the child throughout the child's life as the paramount consideration.

(4) The court or adoption agency must, so far as is reasonably practicable, have regard in particular to—

(a) the value of a stable family unit in the child's development,

(b) the child's ascertainable views regarding the decision (taking account of the child's age and maturity),

(c) the child's religious persuasion, racial origin and cultural and linguistic background, and

(d) the likely effect on the child, throughout the child's life, of the making of an adoption order.

(5) Where an adoption agency is placing a child for adoption it must have regard, so far as is reasonably practicable, to the views of the parents, guardians and other relatives of the child.

(6) In carrying out the duties imposed on it by subsections (2) to (4) an adoption agency must, before making any arrangements for the adoption of a child, consider whether adoption is likely best to meet the needs of

the child or whether there is some better practical alternative for the child.

(7) If an adoption agency concludes that there is an alternative such as is mentioned in subsection (6), it must not make arrangements for the adoption of the child.

(8) Without prejudice to the generality of subsection (4)(b), a child who is aged 12 or over is presumed to be of sufficient age and maturity to form a view for the purposes of that subsection.

PART TWO

PERMANENCE ORDERS

The making of permanence orders

80 Permanence orders

(1) The appropriate court may, on the application of a local authority, make a permanence order in respect of a child.

(2) A permanence order is an order consisting of—

(a) the mandatory provision,

(b) such of the ancillary provisions as the court thinks fit, and

(c) if the conditions in section 83 are met, provision granting authority for the child to be adopted.

(3) In making a permanence order in respect of a child, the appropriate court must secure that each parental responsibility and parental right in respect of the child vests in a person.

81 Permanence orders: mandatory provision

(1) The mandatory provision is provision vesting in the local authority for the appropriate period—

(a) the responsibility mentioned in section 1(1)(b)(ii) of the 1995 Act (provision of guidance appropriate to child's stage of development) in relation to the child, and

(b) the right mentioned in section 2(1)(a) of that Act (regulation of child's residence) in relation to the child.

(2) In subsection (1) *"the appropriate period"* means—

(a) in the case of the responsibility referred to in subsection (1)(a), the period beginning with the making of the permanence order and ending with the day on which the child reaches the age of 18,

(b) in the case of the right referred to in subsection (1)(b), the period beginning with the making of the permanence order and ending with the day on which the child reaches the age of 16.

82 Permanence orders: ancillary provisions

(1) The ancillary provisions are provisions—

(a) vesting in the local authority for the appropriate period—

(i) such of the parental responsibilities mentioned in section 1(1)(a), (b)(i) and (d) of the 1995 Act, and

(ii) such of the parental rights mentioned in section 2(1)(b) and (d) of that Act,

in relation to the child as the court considers appropriate,

(b) vesting in a person other than the local authority for the appropriate period—

(i) such of the parental responsibilities mentioned in section 1(1) of that Act, and

(ii) such of the parental rights mentioned in section 2(1)(b) to (d) of that Act,

in relation to the child as the court considers appropriate,

(c) extinguishing any parental responsibilities which, immediately before the making of the order, vested in a parent or guardian of the child, and which—

(i) by virtue of section 81(1)(a) or paragraph (a)(i), vest in the local authority, or

(ii) by virtue of paragraph (b)(i), vest in a person other than the authority,

(d) extinguishing any parental rights in relation to the child which, immediately before the making of the order, vested in a parent or guardian of the child, and which—

(i) by virtue of paragraph (a)(ii), vest in the local authority, or

(ii) by virtue of paragraph (b)(ii), vest in a person other than the authority,

(e) specifying such arrangements for contact between the child and any other person as the court considers appropriate and to be in the best interests of the child, and

(f) determining any question which has arisen in connection with—

(i) any parental responsibilities or parental rights in relation to the child, or

(ii) any other aspect of the welfare of the child.

(2) In subsection (1), *"the appropriate period"* means—

(a) in the case of the responsibility mentioned in section 1(1)(b)(ii) of the 1995 Act, the period beginning with the making of the permanence order and ending with the day on which the child reaches the age of 18,

(b) in any other case, the period beginning with the making of the permanence order and ending with the day on which the child reaches the age of 16.

84 Conditions and considerations applicable to making of order

(1) Except where subsection (2) applies, a permanence order may not be made in respect of a child who is aged 12 or over unless the child consents.

(2) This subsection applies where the court is satisfied that the child is incapable of consenting to the order.

(3) The court may not make a permanence order in respect of a child unless it considers that it would be better for the child that the order be made than that it should not be made.

(4) In considering whether to make a permanence order and, if so, what provision the order should make, the court is to regard the need to safeguard and promote the welfare of the child throughout childhood as the paramount consideration.

(5) Before making a permanence order, the court must—

(a) after taking account of the child's age and maturity, so far as is reasonably practicable—

(i) give the child the opportunity to indicate whether the child wishes to express any views, and

(ii) if the child does so wish, give the child the opportunity to express them,

(b) have regard to—

(i) any such views the child may express,

(ii) the child's religious persuasion, racial origin and cultural and linguistic background, and

(iii) the likely effect on the child of the making of the order, and

(c) be satisfied that—

(i) there is no person who has the right mentioned in subsection (1)(a) of section 2 of the 1995 Act to have the child living with the person or otherwise to regulate the child's residence, or

(ii) where there is such a person, the child's residence with the person is, or is likely to be, seriously detrimental to the welfare of the child.

(6) A child who is aged 12 or over is presumed to be of sufficient age and maturity to form a view for the purposes of subsection (5)(a).

85 Child in respect of whom order may be made

(1) A permanence order may be made in respect of a child who is an adopted child.

(2) A permanence order may not be made in respect of a child who is or has been—

(a) married,

(b) a civil partner.

86 Representations

(1) In any proceedings relating to an application for a permanence order, the appropriate court must permit any person mentioned in subsection (2) who wishes to make representations to the court to do so.

(2) Those persons are—

(a) the local authority making the application,

(b) the child or the child's representative,

(c) any person who has parental responsibilities or parental rights in relation to the child,

(d) any other person who claims an interest.

Effect of order

87 Effect of order on existing parental right

The making of a permanence order extinguishes the parental right mentioned in subsection (1)(a) of section 2 of the 1995 Act of—

(a) a parent of the child in respect of whom the order is made,

(b) a guardian of such a child,

which, immediately before the making of the order, vested in the parent or, as the case may be, guardian.

88 Effect of order on existing orders

(1) This section applies where—

(a) parental responsibilities or parental rights in relation to a child vest in a person by virtue of—

(i) a permanence order, or

(ii) an order under section 11 of the 1995 Act (court orders relating to parental responsibilities etc.),

("the existing order"), and

(b) the appropriate court intends to make a permanence order ("the new order") as respects the child.

(2) On the making of the new order, the existing order is revoked.

(3) In making the new order, the court must secure that the parental responsibilities or parental rights vesting by virtue of the existing order vest in a person under the new order.

89 [Revocation of compulsory supervision order on making of permanence order]1

(1) Subsection (2) applies where—

(a) the child in respect of whom a permanence order is to be made is subject to a compulsory supervision order , and

(b) the appropriate court is satisfied that, were it to make a permanence order in respect of the child, [it would no longer be necessary that, for the protection, guidance, treatment or control of the child, the child be subject to the compulsory supervision order.]3

(2) The court must make an order providing that, on the making of the permanence order, the [compulsory supervision order]4 ceases to have effect.

90 Precedence of certain other orders

(1) Subsection (2) applies where a local authority has, by virtue of a permanence order, parental responsibilities or parental rights in relation to a child.

(2) The local authority must not act in any way which would be incompatible with—

(a) any other court order of which the authority is aware relating to the child or the child's property,

(b) any [compulsory supervision order or interim compulsory supervision order]2 to which the child is subject.

91 Exercise of parental right under order

(1) Subsection (2) applies where—

(a) two or more persons have a parental right in relation to a child, and

(b) by virtue of paragraph (a) or (b) of subsection (1) of section 82, the right vests in one of them or, as the case may be, two or more of them.

(2) Each of the persons mentioned in subsection (1)(a) may exercise the right without the consent of the other or, as the case may be, any of the others.

(3) Subsection (2) does not apply where an order vesting the right, or regulating its exercise, provides otherwise.

92 Variation of ancillary provisions in order

(1) This section applies where a permanence order which includes ancillary provisions is in force.

(2) The appropriate court may, on an application by a person mentioned in subsection (3), vary such of the ancillary provisions as the court considers appropriate.

(3) Those persons are—

(a) the local authority on whose application the permanence order was made,

(b) if the child in respect of whom the order was made is—

(i) aged 12 or over, or

(ii) under the age of 12 but, in the court's opinion (taking account of the child's age and maturity), capable of understanding the effect of the order,

that child,

(c) any person in whom parental responsibilities and parental rights are vested by virtue of the order,

(d) any person in whom were vested, immediately before the making of the order, any parental responsibilities or parental rights which, by virtue of the making of the order, vest in another person,

(e) any person in whom were vested, immediately before a variation by virtue of this section of the order, parental responsibilities or parental rights which, by virtue of the variation, vest in another person,

(f) any other person who claims an interest.

(4) Subsection (5) applies where the court exercises its power under subsection (2) to vary the ancillary provisions so as to vest, by virtue of paragraph (a) or (b) of subsection (1) of section 82, in a person a parental responsibility or a parental right which, immediately before the variation, vested in another person.

(5) The court may include in the order as varied provision extinguishing the responsibility or right of that other person.

(6) Subsections (4), (5)(a) and (b) and (6) of section 84 apply to the variation of a permanence order under this section as they apply to the making of such an order.

(7) In subsections (1) and (2), *"ancillary provisions"* has the same meaning as in section 82.

(8) In this section, *"vary"* includes add to, omit, or amend; and *"variation"* is to be construed accordingly.

93 Amendment of order to grant authority for child to be adopted

(1) This section applies where—

(a) a permanence order in respect of a child is in force, and

(b) the order does not include provision granting authority for the child to be adopted.

(2) On the application of the local authority on whose application the order was made, the appropriate court may amend the order so as to include provision granting authority for the child to be adopted if (and only if)—

(a) the court is satisfied that the child has been placed for adoption, or is likely to be placed for adoption,

(b) the court is satisfied that the condition in subsection (3) or subsection (4) is met, and

(c) the court considers that it would be better for the child that authority for the child to be adopted is granted than that it should not be granted.

(3) The condition is that each parent or guardian of the child understands what the effect of making an adoption order would be and consents to the making of such an order in relation to the child.

(4) The condition is that the consent of each parent or guardian should be dispensed with on any of the grounds mentioned in section 83.

(5) Subsections (4), (5)(a) and (b) and (6) of section 84 apply to the amendment of a permanence order under this section as they apply to the making of such an order.

(6) In subsections (3) and (4)—

"guardian", in relation to a child in respect of whom a permanence order to which this section applies is in force, means a guardian—

(a) who has any parental responsibilities or parental rights in relation to the child, or

(b) who, by virtue of the making of a previous such order, no longer has any such responsibilities or rights,

"parent", in relation to a child in respect of whom a permanence order to which this section applies is in force, means a parent—

(a) who has any parental responsibilities or parental rights in relation to the child, or

(b) who, by virtue of the making of a previous such order, no longer has any such responsibilities or rights.

94 Proceedings

(1) In any proceedings for variation of a permanence order by the local authority on whose application the order was granted, the appropriate court must permit any person who is affected by the order, and who wishes to make representations to the court, to do so.

(2) In any proceedings for variation of a permanence order by a person other than the local authority on whose application the order was granted, the appropriate court must permit any person mentioned in subsection (3) who wishes to make representations to the court to do so.

(3) Those persons are—

(a) the local authority on whose application the permanence order was made,

(b) if the child in respect of whom the original order was made is—

(i) aged 12 or over, or

(ii) under the age of 12 but, in the court's opinion (taking account of the child's age and maturity), is capable of understanding the effect of the order,

that child,

(c) any person who has parental responsibilities or parental rights in relation to the child,

(d) any person on whom a duty was imposed, or power conferred, by the order,

(e) any person in whom were vested, immediately before the making of the order, any parental responsibilities or parental rights which, by virtue of the making of the order, vest in another person,

(f) any person in whom were vested, immediately before a variation by virtue of section 92 of the order, parental responsibilities or parental rights which, by virtue of the variation, vest in another person, and

(g) any other person who claims an interest.

95 Duty of children's hearing to prepare report for court

(1) Subsection (2) applies where—

(a) an application is made for a permanence order, or variation of such an order, in respect of a child,

(b) the application has not been determined (or, as the case may be, withdrawn or abandoned), and

(c) a children's hearing proposes to [make or vary (other than by interim variation, as defined in section 140 of the Children's Hearing (Scotland) Act 2011 (asp 1)) a compulsory supervision order in respect of the child.

(2) The children's hearing must prepare for the court to which the application has been made a report containing such information as the Scottish Ministers may by regulations prescribe.

(3) In subsection (1)(a), the reference to variation of a permanence order includes a reference to amendment of the order to include provision granting authority for the child to whom the order relates to be adopted.

96 Application: effect on compulsory supervision order

(1) Subsection (2) applies where an application is made for a permanence order, or variation of such an order, in respect of a child.

(2) [A compulsory supervision order may not be made or varied (other than by interim variation, as defined in section 140 of the Children's Hearings (Scotland) Act 2011 (asp 1)) in respect of the child, until the application is determined (or, as the case may be, withdrawn or abandoned).

(3) Subsection (2) does not apply if the court to which the application is made refers the child's case to the Principal Reporter (whether following receipt of a report under section 95 or otherwise).

(4) In subsection (1), the reference to variation of a permanence order includes a reference to amendment of the order to include provision granting authority for the child to whom the order relates to be adopted.

97 [Interim orders and revocation of compulsory supervision order]1

(1) Subsection (2) applies where an application is made for a permanence order, or variation of such an order, in respect of a child.

(2) The appropriate court may make such interim order as it thinks fit.

(3) Subsection (4) applies where—

(a) the child in respect of whom an interim order is to be made is subject to a [compulsory supervision order]2 , and

(b) the court is satisfied that, were it to make an interim order in relation to the child, [it would no longer be necessary that, for the protection, guidance, treatment or control of the child, the child be subject to the compulsory supervision order.]3

(4) The court must make an order providing that, on the making of the interim order, the [compulsory supervision order]4 ceases to have effect.

(5) If—

(a) the child in respect of whom an interim order is made is subject to a compulsory supervision order , and

(b) the provisions of the [interim order conflict, or are otherwise inconsistent, with the compulsory supervision order,

the provisions of the interim order prevail.

(6) In subsection (1), the reference to variation of a permanence order includes a reference to amendment of the order to include provision granting authority for the child to whom the order relates to be adopted.

98 Revocation

(1) The appropriate court may, on an application by a person mentioned in subsection (2), revoke a permanence order if satisfied that it is appropriate to do so in all the circumstances of the case, including, in particular—

(a) a material change in the circumstances directly relating to any of the order's provisions,

(b) any wish by the parent or guardian of the child in respect of whom the order was made to have reinstated any parental responsibilities or parental rights vested in another person by virtue of the order.

(2) Those persons are—

(a) the local authority on whose application the order was made,

(b) any other person affected by the order who has obtained the leave of the court to apply for revocation of the order.

(3) Subsections (4), (5)(a) and (b) and (6) of section 84 apply to the revocation of a permanence order under this section as they apply to the making of such an order.

99 Duty of local authority to apply for variation or revocation

(1) Subsection (2) applies where a local authority on whose application a permanence order was made determines that—

(a) there has been a material change in the circumstances directly relating to any of the order's provisions, and

(b) in consequence of that change, the order ought to be varied or revoked.

(2) The authority must, as soon as is reasonably practicable, apply to the appropriate court for variation or, as the case may be, revocation of the order.

(3) In this section, *"variation"*, in relation to the permanence order, includes amendment of the order so as to include provision granting authority for the child to whom the order relates to be adopted; and *"varied"* is to be construed accordingly.

100 Revocation: order under section 11 of 1995 Act

(1) Subsection (2) applies where the appropriate court revokes a permanence order in respect of a child.

(2) The court must consider whether to make an order under section 11 of the 1995 Act—

(a) imposing on a person specified in the order parental responsibilities in relation to the child, and

(b) giving to such a person parental rights in relation to the child.

101 Local authority to give notice of certain matters

(1) This section applies where—

(a) a permanence order includes provision granting authority for the child to be adopted,

(b) after the order is made or, as the case may be, amended under section 93(2) so as to include that provision, an event mentioned in subsection (2) occurs, and

(c) the order has not been revoked under section 98(1).

(2) Those events are—

(a) the child is placed for adoption,

(b) an adoption order is made in respect of the child,

(c) the child ceases to be placed for adoption otherwise than on the making of an adoption order.

(3) As soon as is reasonably practicable after the occurrence of the event, the local authority on whose application the permanence order was made must give notice of the event to any person falling within subsection (4).

(4) A person falls within this subsection if—

(a) the person consented under section 83(1)(c)(i) or 93(3) to the making of the order,

(b) the person's consent to the making of the order was dispensed with under section 83(1)(c)(ii) or 93(4).

(5) The local authority need not comply with the requirement imposed by subsection (3) in relation to a person if the person has given notice to that effect to the authority.

102 Effect of subsequent adoption order on permanence order

(1) Subsection (2) applies where—

(a) a permanence order is in force in respect of a child, and

(b) an adoption order is made in respect of the child.

(2) The permanence order ceases to have effect on the making of the adoption order.

103 Restriction on making of orders under section 11 of 1995 Act

After section 11 of the 1995 Act insert the following section—

"11A Restriction on making of orders under section 11

(1) Subsection (2) applies where a permanence order (as defined in section 80(2) of the Adoption and Children (Scotland) Act 2007 (asp 4)) is in force in respect of a child.

(2) The court may not, under subsection (1) of section 11 of this Act, make an order such as is mentioned in any of paragraphs (a) to (e) of subsection (2) of that section.".

APPENDIX TWO

RULES OF THE COURT OF SESSION – CHAPTER 67

PART 4

PERMANENCE ORDERS

Application for permanence order

67.28—(1) An application for a permanence order under section 80 of the 2007 Act is to be made by petition in Form 67.28.

(2) The following documents must be lodged in process along with a petition under paragraph (1):—

(a) an extract of the entry in the Register of Births relating to the child who is the subject of the application;

(b) a report by the petitioner in numbered paragraphs which deals with the following matters:—

(i) how the needs of the child came to the notice of the petitioner;

(ii) any relevant family circumstances of the child;

(iii) a description of the physical and mental health of the child (including any special needs) and his emotional, behavioural and educational development;

(iv) an account of the discussion by the petitioner with the parents or guardians of the child and, if appropriate, with the child about their wishes and the alternatives to a permanence order;

(v) where appropriate, whether the father of the child has been given notice and provided with the prescribed information under section 105(2) of the 2007 Act;

(vi) the knowledge of the petitioner of the position of other relatives or persons likely to be involved;

(vii) an account of the search by the petitioner for any parent or guardian who cannot be found;

(viii) the arrangements of the petitioner to care for the child after the making of a permanence order (including the arrangements for contact between the child and any other person);

(ix) the child's religious persuasion, racial origin and cultural and linguistic background;

(x) the likely effect on the child of the making of a permanence order;

(xi) whether there is a person who has the right mentioned in section 2(1)(a) of the 1995 Act to have the child living with the person or otherwise to regulate the child's residence and, where there is such a person, evidence that the child's residence with the person is or is likely to be seriously detrimental to the welfare of the child;

(xii) whether the child is or has been married or a civil partner;

(xiii) in the case of a petition containing a request that the order include provision granting authority for the child to be adopted, the matters mentioned in paragraph (3);

(xiv) in the case of a petition in respect of a child who is aged 12 or over, whether the child consents to the making of the order or is incapable of doing so;

(xv) whether the child is subject to a supervision requirement under section 70 of the 1995 Act;

(xvi) any other information which may be of assistance to the court having regard, in particular, to sections 83 (if appropriate) and 84 of the 2007 Act;

(c) any other document founded upon by the petitioner in support of the terms of the petition.

(3) The matters referred to in paragraph (2)(xiii) are—

(a) whether the child has been, or is likely to be, placed for adoption;

(b) whether each parent or guardian of the child understands what the effect of making an adoption order would be and consents to the making of such an order in relation to the child, or the grounds on which such consent should be dispensed with.

(4) If the report mentioned in paragraph (2)(b) is unavailable to be lodged with the petition, the court shall pronounce an interlocutor requiring the petitioner to prepare and lodge such a report within 2 weeks of the date of the interlocutor, or within such other period as the court in its discretion may allow.

Appointment of curator ad litem and reporting officer

67.29.—(1) The court must, on the lodging of a petition under rule 67.28 appoint a curator *ad litem* and reporting officer.

(2) Subject to paragraph (3), the court must not appoint a reporting officer where the petition does not request that the order include provision granting authority for the child to be adopted.

(3) Notwithstanding paragraph (2), a reporting officer must be appointed where the child who is the subject of the application is aged 12 or over for the purpose of witnessing that child's consent where that consent is to be executed in Scotland.

(4) The same person may be appointed as curator ad litem and reporting officer in the same petition if the court considers that doing so is appropriate in the circumstances.

(5) A person may, before presenting the petition, apply by letter to the Deputy Principal Clerk for the appointment of a reporting officer.

(6) An application under paragraph (4) shall—

(a) set out the reasons for which the appointment is sought;

(b) not require to be intimated to any person;

(c) be accompanied by an interlocutor sheet; and

(d) be placed by the Deputy Principal Clerk before the Lord Ordinary for his decision.

(7) The Deputy Principal Clerk shall intimate the appointment of a curator ad litem and reporting officer under paragraph (1) or (5) to the petitioner and to the person or persons appointed.

(8) The decision of the Lord Ordinary on an application under paragraph (5) shall be final and not subject to review.

(9) The letter and the interlocutor sheet in an application under paragraph (5) shall be kept in the Petition Department and subsequently placed in the process of the petition.

Intimation of application

67.30.—(1) On the lodging of a petition under rule 67.28—

(a) the Deputy Principal Clerk must cause the petition to be put on the By Order Roll before the Lord Ordinary not less than 6 and not more than 8 weeks thereafter;

(b) where the petition does not contain a request that the order include provision granting authority for the child to be adopted, the petitioner must intimate a copy of the petition along with a notice of intimation in Form 67.30-A to—

(i) any person who has parental responsibilities or parental rights in relation to the child; and

(ii) any person who claims to have an interest;

(c) where the petition contains such a request—

(i) the petitioner must intimate a copy of the petition along with a notice of intimation in Form 67.30-A to the persons mentioned in paragraph (2); and

(ii) the petitioner must intimate a copy of the petition along with a notice of intimation in Form 67.30-B to the father of the child if he does not have, and never has had, parental responsibilities and parental rights in relation to the child;

(d) the Deputy Principal Clerk must intimate the date of the hearing on the By Order Roll to the curator ad litem and to any reporting officer appointed under rule 67.29;

(e) the court may order the petitioner to intimate the application to such other person as it considers appropriate.

(2) The persons referred to in paragraph (1)(c)(i) are

(a) every person who can be found and whose consent to the making of the order is required to be given or dispensed with under the 2007 Act;

(b) if no such person can be found, a relative of the child within the meaning of section 119(1) of the 2007 Act unless the address of such a relative is not known to the petitioner and cannot reasonably be ascertained.

(3) A notice of intimation under paragraph (1)(c)(i) must include the following matters:–

(a) that an application for a permanence order containing a request that the order include provision granting authority for the child to be adopted has been made;

(b) the date on which and place where the By Order hearing will be held;

(c) the fact that the person is entitled to be heard on the application;

(d) the fact that, unless the person wishes, or the court requires, the person need not attend the hearing.

(4) A notice of intimation under paragraph (1)(c)(ii) must include the matters mentioned in paragraphs (3)(a) and (b).

Hearing on the By Order Roll

67.31.—(1) At the By Order hearing appointed under rule 67.30 the court must—

(a) if no party indicates his intention to oppose the petition, dispose of the cause or make such other order as it considers appropriate; or

(b) in any other case—

(i) ascertain from the parties the anticipated length of any proof that may be required;

(ii) fix a diet of proof not less than 12 and not more than 16 weeks after the date of the hearing on the By Order Roll unless, on cause shown, a longer period is appropriate;

(iii) give such directions as to the preparation for the proof as it considers appropriate;

(iv) order answers and any other documents to be lodged within 21 days of the date of the hearing on the By Order Roll or such other period as it considers appropriate.

(2) Paragraph (1)(b)(ii) shall not require a proof to be held when the court is in vacation unless the court otherwise directs.

(3) At the By Order hearing the court may—

(a) if it is not satisfied that the facts stated in the petition are supported by the documents lodged with it or by the reports of the curator ad litem and reporting officer, order the production of further documents; and

(b) where it considers it appropriate to do so, fix a pre-proof hearing not less than 2 and not more than 6 weeks before the diet of proof;

(c) make such other order as it considers appropriate for the expeditious progress of the case.

Pre-proof hearing

67.32.—(1) If the court appoints a pre-proof hearing under rule 67.31, the parties must provide the court with sufficient information to enable it to conduct the hearing as provided for in this rule.

(2) At the pre-proof hearing the court must ascertain, so far as is reasonably practicable, whether the cause is likely to proceed to proof on the date fixed for that purpose and, in particular, the court must consider—

(a) the state of preparation of the parties;

(b) the extent to which the parties have complied with any orders made by the court under rule 67.31.

(3) At the pre-proof hearing the court may—

(a) discharge the proof and fix a new date for such proof;

(b) adjourn the pre-proof hearing;

(c) order the lodging of joint minutes of agreement, affidavits and expert reports within such period as it considers appropriate;

(d) make such other order as it considers appropriate to secure the expeditious progress of the cause.

Final procedure

67.33.—(1) Where a permanence order has been granted, the Deputy Principal Clerk must—

(a) after the expiry of 14 days from the date of, or date of confirmation of, the order without an appeal having been taken, issue an extract of the order to the petitioner;

(b) where the court has also made an order under section 89(2) (revocation of supervision requirement) of the 2007 Act, intimate the making of that order to the Principal Reporter.

(2) Where the permanence order includes provision granting authority for the child to be adopted, the Deputy Principal Clerk must, after complying with paragraph (1), seal the process in an envelope marked "Confidential".

(3) The envelope referred to in paragraph (2) must not be unsealed by the clerk of court or any other person having control of the records of that or any court, and the process shall not be made accessible to any person for one hundred years after the date of the granting of the order except—

(a) to the person to whom the permanence order relates once he has attained the age of 16 years;

(b) to the Deputy Principal Clerk, on an application made to him by an adoption agency, with the consent of the person to whom the process relates, for the purpose only of ascertaining the name of the agency, if any, responsible for the placement of that person and informing the applicant of that name;

(c) to a person, on an application made by him to the court setting forth the reasons for which access to the process is required;

(d) to a court, public authority or administrative board (whether in the United Kingdom or not) having power to authorise an adoption, on petition by it to the court which granted the original order requesting that information be made available from the process for the purpose of discharging its duties in considering an application for adoption and specifying the precise reasons for which access to the process is required; or

(e) to a person who is authorised by the Scottish Ministers to obtain information from the process for the purpose of such research as is intended to improve the working of adoption law and practice.

Variation of ancillary provisions in order

67.34—(1) An application under section 92(2) of the 2007 Act (application for variation of ancillary provisions) is to be made by note.

(2) A note under paragraph (1) must contain—

(a) the name and address of the applicant;

(b) the applicant's relationship to and interest in the child;

(c) the name and address of the local authority on whose application the permanence order was granted;

(d) details of the original application;

(e) details of any other person affected by the order;

(f) the grounds on which variation is sought;

(g) details of whether the child is subject to a supervision requirement under section 70 of the 1995 Act;

(h) details of the order sought by the applicant.

(3) On presentation of a note under paragraph (1) the court must

(a) order the applicant to intimate the note to—

(i) the petitioner in the original application, where it is not the applicant;

(ii) any other person affected by the order; and

(iii) such other persons as the court considers appropriate; and

(b) appoint a curator ad litem.

(4) Any person to whom intimation is given under paragraph (2) may, within 14 days after the date on which intimation is made, lodge answers to the note.

(5) Where answers have been lodged under paragraph (4) the court must order a hearing to be fixed.

(6) Where no answers have been lodged under paragraph (4) the court may order a hearing to be fixed.

(7) Where the court orders a hearing to be fixed under paragraph (5) or (6) it may also order a pre-proof hearing to be fixed not less than 2 and not more than 6 weeks before the hearing.

(8) Rule 67.32 is to apply, with any necessary modifications, to any pre-proof hearing fixed under paragraph (7).

(9) The court shall order the applicant to intimate any hearing fixed under paragraph (5), (6) or

(7) to the petitioner in the original application, where it is not the applicant, to any other person affected by the order and to such other persons as the court considers appropriate.

Amendment of order to grant authority for child to be adopted

67.35.—(1) An application under section 93(2) (amendment of order to include provision granting authority for child to be adopted) of the 2007 Act is to be made by note.

(2) A note under paragraph (1) must contain—

(a) the name and address of the applicant;

(b) details of the original application;

(c) details of the following matters:–

(i) whether the child has been, or is likely to be, placed for adoption;

(ii) whether each parent or guardian of the child understands what the effect of making an adoption order would be and consents to the making of such an order in relation to the child, or the grounds on which such consent should be dispensed with;

(iii) the child's religious persuasion, racial origin and cultural and linguistic background;

(iv) whether the child is subject to a supervision requirement under section 70 of the 1995 Act;

(v) the likely effect on the child of the making of the order.

(3) On the lodging of a note under paragraph (1)—

(a) the Deputy Principal Clerk must cause the note to be put on the By Order Roll before the Lord Ordinary not less than 6 and not more than 8 weeks after the date of lodging the application;

(b) the applicant must intimate a copy of the note along with a notice of intimation in Form 67.35-A to every person who can be found and whose consent to the making of the order is required to be given or dispensed with under the 2007 Act;

(c) the applicant must intimate a copy of the note along with a notice of intimation in Form 67.35-B to the father of the child if he does not have, and never has had, parental responsibilities in relation to the child;

(d) the court may order the applicant to intimate the note to such other persons as it considers appropriate;

(e) the court must appoint a curator ad litem and reporting officer and the same person may be appointed as curator ad litem and reporting officer if the court considers that doing so is appropriate in the circumstances.

(4) A notice of intimation under paragraph (3)(b) must state the following matters:–

(a) that an application has been made;

(b) the date on which, and place where, the By Order hearing will be heard;

(c) the fact that the person is entitled to be heard on the application;

(d) the fact that, unless the person wishes, or the court requires, the person need not attend the hearing.

(5) A notice of intimation under paragraph (3)(c) must state the matters mentioned in paragraph (4)(a) and (b).

(6) Rules 67.31 to 67.33 are to apply, with any necessary modifications, to an application under this rule and they apply to an application under rule 67.28

Revocation

67.36.—(1) An application under section 98(1) (revocation of a permanence order) of the 2007 Act shall be made by note.

(2) A note under paragraph (1) must contain—

(a) the name and address of the applicant;

(b) the applicant's relationship to and interest in the child;

(c) the name and address of the local authority on whose application the permanence order was granted;

(d) details of the original application;

(e) details of any other person affected by the order;

(f) the grounds on which revocation is sought;

(g) details of whether the child is subject to a supervision requirement under section 70 of the 1995 Act;

(h) details of the order sought by the applicant;

(i) detailed proposals for the future welfare of the child.

(3) On the lodging of a note under paragraph (1), the court must—

(a) order the applicant to intimate the note to—

(i) the petitioner in the original application, where it is not the applicant;

(ii) any other person affected by the order; and

(iii) such other persons as he considers appropriate; and

(b) appoint a curator *ad litem*.

(4) Any person to whom intimation has been given under paragraph (3) may, within 14 days after the date on which intimation is made, lodge answers to the note.

(5) Where answers have been lodged under paragraph (4), the court must order a hearing to be fixed.

(6) Where no answers have been lodged under paragraph (4) the court may—

(a) order the relevant local authority to submit a report to him;

(b) order a hearing to be fixed;

(c) order both such a report and such a hearing.

(7) Where the court orders a hearing to be fixed under paragraph (5) or (6) it may also order a pre-proof hearing to be fixed not less than 2 and not more than 6 weeks before the hearing.

(8) Rule 67.32 is to apply, with any necessary modifications, to any pre-proof hearing fixed under paragraph (7).

(9) The court shall order the applicant to intimate any hearing fixed under paragraph (5), (6) or

(7) to the petitioner in the original application, where it is not the applicant, to any other person affected by the order and to such other persons as the court considers appropriate.

(10)An order made in respect of an application under paragraph (1) may specify the person—

(a) on whom parental responsibilities are imposed in consequence of the making of the order; and

(b) to whom parental rights are given in consequence of the making of the order.

Protection of address of child

67.37—(1) Where an applicant under this Part wishes to prevent the address of the child being disclosed to any person whose consent to the making of an order is required, the applicant may apply to the Deputy Principal Clerk for a serial number to be assigned for that purpose.

(2) On receipt of an application under paragraph (1) the Deputy Principal Clerk must—

(a) assign a serial number in respect of the child's address; and

(b) enter a note of the number opposite the child's address in a register of serial numbers.

(3) The contents of the register of serial numbers and the addresses of the children to whom each number relates shall be treated as confidential by the sheriff clerk and are not to be disclosed to any person other than the sheriff.

(4) Where a serial number has been assigned under paragraph (2), any form of consent to a permanence order—

(a) must refer to the child's address by means of the serial number assigned to it; and

(b) must specify the year in which and the court by which the serial number was assigned.

Duties of reporting officer and curator ad litem

67.38.—(1) The other duties of a reporting officer appointed under this Part, other than under rule 67.29(3), which are prescribed for the purposes of section 108(1)(b) of the 2007 Act are—

(a) to ascertain the whereabouts of all persons whose consent to the making of an adoption order in respect of the child is required;

(b) to ascertain whether there is any person other than those mentioned in the petition upon whom notice of the petition should be served;

(c) in the case of each person whose consent to the making of an adoption order is required or may be dispensed with—

(i) to ascertain whether that person understands what the effect of making an adoption order would be;

(ii) to ascertain whether alternatives to adoption have been discussed with that person;

(iii) to confirm that that person understands that he may withdraw his consent at any time before an order is made;

(d) to confirm that each parent or guardian of the child who can be found is aware that he may apply to the court for—

(i) variation of the ancillary provisions in the permanence order under section 92 of the 2007 Act; and

(ii) revocation of a permanence order under section 98 of the 2007 Act, and of the appropriate procedure for these applications.

(e) to report in writing on the matters mentioned in subparagraphs (a) to (d) to the court within 4 weeks from date of interlocutor appointing the reporting officer, or within such other period as the court may allow.

(2) References in paragraph (1) to "consent" are to consent within the meaning of section 83(1)(c), 84(1) or 93(3) of the 2007 Act as the case may be.

(3) A curator ad litem appointed under this Part must—

(a) have regard to safeguarding the interests of the child as his paramount duty;

(b) inquire, so far as he considers necessary into the facts and circumstances stated in the petition or minute, as the case may be, and in any report lodged under rule 31(2)(b);

(c) where appropriate, establish the child's religious persuasion, racial origin and cultural and linguistic background;

(d) where appropriate, establish whether the order is likely to safeguard and promote the welfare of the child throughout childhood;

(e) ascertain whether the child is subject to a supervision requirement under section 70 of the 1995 Act;

(f) ascertain from the child whether he wishes to express a view and, where the child indicates his wish to express a view, ascertain that view;

(g) ascertain the likely effect on the child of the making of the order;

(h) where appropriate, ascertain whether it would be better for the child that the order be made than that it should not be made;

(i) where appropriate, ascertain whether it would be better for the child if the court were to grant authority for the child to be adopted than if it were not to grant such authority;

(j) where appropriate, ascertain whether the child has been, or is likely to be, placed for adoption.

(4) Subject to paragraph (5) the curator ad litem must report in writing on the matters mentioned in paragraph (3) to the court within 4 weeks from the date of the interlocutor appointing the curator, or within such other period as the court may allow.

(5) Subject to any order made by the court under rule 67.40 the views of the child ascertained in terms of paragraph (3)(f) may, if the curator ad litem considers appropriate, be conveyed to the court orally.

Consents

67.39.—(1) The consent of a parent or guardian required by section 83(1)(c) or 93(3) of the 2007 Act is to be in Form 67.39-A.

(2) The consent of the child required under section 84(1) of the 2007 Act is to be in Form 67.39-B.

(3) A form of consent mentioned in paragraph (1) or (2) must be witnessed—

(a) where it is executed in Scotland, by the reporting officer appointed under this Part;

(b) where it is executed outwith Scotland but within the United Kingdom, by a justice of the peace or commissioner for oaths; or

(c) where it is executed outwith the United Kingdom—

(i) if the person who executes the form is serving in Her Majesty's forces, by an officer holding a commission in any of those forces; or

(ii) in any other case, by a British diplomatic or consular official or any person authorised to administer an oath or affirmation under the law of the place where the consent is executed.

Procedure where child wishes to express a view

67.40.—(1) Where a child has indicated his wish to express his views the court, without prejudice to rule 67.38(3)(f)—

(a) may order such procedural steps to be taken as it considers appropriate to ascertain the views of that child; and

(b) must not make an order under this Part unless an opportunity has been given for the views of that child to be obtained or heard.

(2) Where the views of a child, whether obtained under this rule or under rule 67.38(2)(f), have been recorded in writing, the court may direct that such a written record is to—

(a) be sealed in a envelope marked "Views of the child – confidential";

(b) be available to the court only;

(c) not be opened by any other person; and

(d) not form a borrowable part of the process.

Procedure where leave of court required

67.41.—(1) Where leave of the court is required under section 94(4) or 98(2)(b) of the 2007 Act before an application for variation or revocation of a permanence order may be made, the applicant must lodge along with the note a motion stating the grounds upon which leave is sought.

(2) A motion under paragraph (1) shall not be served or intimated unless the court otherwise directs.

(3) The court may hear the applicant on the motion and may grant or refuse it or make such other order in relation to it as it considers appropriate prior to determination.

(4) Where such motion is granted, a copy of the interlocutor shall be intimated along with the note of application.

Intimation to Principal Reporter

67.42. Where an application under this Part is made in respect of a child whose case has been referred to a children's hearing or who is subject to a supervision requirement under the 1995 Act, the Deputy Principal Clerk shall intimate the fact that the application has been made to the Principal Reporter.

Report of children's hearing

67.43.—(1) On receipt of a report from a children's hearing under section 95(2) of the 2007 Act the Deputy Principal Clerk shall—

(a) lodge the report in the process of the application; and

(b) send a copy of the report together with a notice in Form 67.43-A to—

(i) the parties to the application;

(ii) any relevant person in relation to the child within the meaning given by section 93(2) of the 1995 Act; and

(iii) such other person as the court considers appropriate.

(2) Any person who receives notice under paragraph (1)(b) and who wishes to oppose the proposals of the children's hearing must lodge a form of response in Form 67.43-B within 7 days of the date notice was given.

(3) Thereafter the court shall consider the report and any form of response lodged under paragraph (2) and decide whether to refer the child's case to the Principal Reporter as mentioned in section 96(3) of the 2007 Act.

(4) Where the court decides to refer the child's case to the Principal Reporter as mentioned in section 96(3) of the 2007 Act, the court shall pronounce an order to this effect which shall narrate in terms that the court is referring the child's case to the Principal Reporter as mentioned in that provision.

(5) Where the court decides not to refer the child's case to the Principal Reporter, it may nevertheless make such other order it considers appropriate for the expeditious progress of the case.

(6) In order to assist it to decide what to do under paragraph (3), the court may order the

holding f a hearing.

(7) If the court so decides, it shall fix a date for the hearing which shall be not more than 7 days after the date of the order.

(8) The Deputy Principal Clerk of Session shall intimate any hearing under paragraph (6) to—

(a) the parties to the application;

(b) any person who lodged a form of response under paragraph (2);

(c) any relevant person in relation to the child within the meaning given by section 93(2) of the 1995 Act; and

(d) such other person as the court considers appropriate.

(9) The court may allow a continuation of a hearing under paragraph (6) on two occasions only, each for a period not exceeding 14 days.

(10)After the court has made its decision under paragraph (3), the Deputy Principal Clerk of Session shall send a notice in Form 67.43-C to the Principal Reporter.

Interim orders

67.44.—(1) An application for an interim order under section 97 of the 2007 Act is to be made by motion

APPENDIX THREE

ACT OF SEDERUNT (SHERIFF COURT RULES AMENDMENT) (ADOPTION AND CHILDREN (SCOTLAND) ACT 2007) 2009 NO. 284

Application for permanence order

31.—(1) An application for a permanence order under section 80 of the 2007 Act is to be made by petition in Form 11.

(2) The following documents must be lodged in process along with a petition under paragraph (1):—

(a) an extract of the entry in the Register of Births relating to the child who is the subject of the application;

(b) a report by the petitioner in numbered paragraphs, if available, which deals with the following matters:—

(i) how the needs of the child came to the notice of the petitioner;

(ii) any relevant family circumstances of the child;

(iii) a description of the physical and mental health of the child (including any special needs) and his emotional, behavioural and educational development;

(iv) an account of the discussion by the petitioner with the parents or guardians of the child and, if appropriate, with the child about their wishes and the alternatives to a permanence order;

(v) where appropriate, whether the father of the child has been given notice and provided with the prescribed information under section 105(2) of the 2007 Act;

(vi) the knowledge of the petitioner of the position of other relatives or persons likely to be involved;

(vii) an account of the search by the petitioner for any parent or guardian who cannot be found;

(viii) the arrangements of the petitioner to care for the child after the making of a permanence order (including the arrangements for contact between the child and any other person);

(ix) the child's religious persuasion, racial origin and cultural and linguistic background;

(x) the likely effect on the child of the making of a permanence order;

(xi) whether there is a person who has the right mentioned in section 2(1)(a) of the 1995 Act to have the child living with the person or otherwise to regulate the child's residence and, where there is such a person, evidence that the child's residence with the person is or is likely to be seriously detrimental to the welfare of the child;

(xii) whether the child is or has been married or a civil partner;

(xiii) in the case of a petition containing a request that the order include provision granting authority for the child to be adopted, the matters mentioned in paragraph (3);

(xiv) in the case of a petition in respect of a child who is aged 12 or over, whether the child consents to the making of the order or is incapable of doing so;

(xv) whether the child is subject to a supervision requirement under section 70 of the 1995 Act;

(xvi) any other information which may be of assistance to the court having regard, in particular, to sections 83 (if appropriate) and 84 of the 2007 Act;

(c) any other document founded upon by the petitioner in support of the terms of the petition.

(3) The matters referred to in paragraph (2)(xiii) are—

(a) whether the child has been, or is likely to be, placed for adoption;

(b) whether each parent or guardian of the child understands what the effect of making an adoption order would be and consents to the making of such an order in relation to the child, or the grounds on which such consent should be dispensed with.

(4) If the report mentioned in paragraph (2)(b) is unavailable to be lodged with the petition, the sheriff shall pronounce an interlocutor requiring the petitioner to prepare and lodge such a report within 2 weeks of the date of the interlocutor, or within such other period as the sheriff in his discretion may allow.

Appointment of curator *ad litem* and reporting officer

32. (1) The sheriff must, on the lodging of a petition under rule 31 appoint a curator *ad litem* and reporting officer.

(2) But, subject to paragraph (3) the sheriff is not to appoint a reporting officer where the petition does not request that the order include provision granting authority for the child to be adopted.

(3) Notwithstanding paragraph (2), a reporting officer must be appointed where the child who is the subject of the application is aged 12 or over for the purpose of witnessing that child's consent where that consent is to be executed in Scotland.

(4) The same person may be appointed as curator *ad litem* and reporting officer in the same petition, if the sheriff considers that doing so is appropriate in the circumstances.

(5) The sheriff may appoint a person who is not a member of a panel established under regulations made by virtue of section 101 of the 1995 Act to be curator *ad litem* or a reporting officer.

(6) The sheriff may, on cause shown, appoint a reporting officer prior to the lodging of a petition.

(7) An application for an appointment under paragraph (6) is to be made by letter addressed to the sheriff clerk specifying the reasons for the appointment, and shall not require to be intimated to any other person.

(8) The sheriff clerk must intimate the appointment of a curator *ad litem* and reporting officer under paragraph (1) or (6) to the person or persons appointed.

Intimation of application

33. (1) On the lodging of a petition under rule 31—

(a) the sheriff clerk must fix a date for a preliminary hearing, which must take place (except on cause shown) not less than 6 and not more than 8 weeks after the date of lodging the petition;

(b) where the petition does not contain a request that the order include provision granting authority for the child to be adopted, the petitioner must send a service copy of the petition in Form 11A along with a notice of intimation in Form 12 to—

(i) any person who has parental responsibilities or parental rights in relation to the child;

(ii) any person who claims to have an interest;

(c) where the petition contains such a request—

(i) the petitioner must send a service copy of the petition in Form 11A along with a notice of intimation in Form 12 to the persons mentioned in paragraph (2); and

(ii) the petitioner must send a service copy of the petition in Form 11A along with a notice of intimation in Form 13 to the father of the child if he does not have, and never has had, parental responsibilities and parental rights in relation to the child;

(d) the sheriff clerk must intimate the date of the preliminary hearing to the curator *ad litem* and to any reporting officer appointed under rule 32;

(e) the sheriff may order the petitioner to intimate the application to such other person and in such terms as he considers appropriate.

(2) The persons referred to in paragraph (1)(c)(i) are—

(a) every person who can be found and whose consent to the making of the order is required to be given or dispensed with under the 2007 Act;

(b) if no such person can be found, a relative of the child within the meaning of section 119(1) of the 2007 Act unless the address of such a relative is not known to the petitioner and cannot reasonably be ascertained.

(3) A notice of intimation under paragraph (1)(c)(i) must include the following matters:—

(a) that an application for a permanence order containing a request that the order include provision granting authority for the child to be adopted has been made;

(b) the date on which and place where the preliminary hearing will be held;

(c) the fact that the person is entitled to be heard on the application;

(d) the fact that, unless the person wishes, or the court requires, the person need not attend the hearing.

(4) A notice of intimation under paragraph (1)(c)(ii) must include the matters mentioned in paragraphs (3)(a) and (b).

(5) The sheriff clerk or petitioner on making intimation shall complete a certificate of intimation in Form 14.

Form of response

34. (1) Any person who has received intimation of an application for a permanence order under rule 33 and who intends to oppose that

application must lodge a form of response in Form 15 not later than 21 days after the date of intimation of the application.

(2) A form of response lodged under paragraph (1) must be intimated by the respondent to the petitioner at the time of lodging.

Opposed applications

34A. Within 14 days of a form of response being lodged, the petitioner shall lodge and intimate to all other parties a brief statement in numbered paragraphs setting out the facts upon which the petitioner intends to rely including averments in relation to—

(a) considerations under section 14 of the 2007 Act;

(b) ancillary provisions under section 82 of the 2007 Act;

(c) conditions under section 83 of the 2007 Act;

(d) conditions and considerations under section 84 of the 2007 Act.

Preliminary hearing

35. (1) At the preliminary hearing the sheriff must—

(a) if no form of response has been lodged under rule 34, dispose of the case or make such other order as he considers appropriate;

(b) if a form of response has been lodged—

(i) ascertain the nature of the issues in dispute, including any questions of admissibility of evidence or any legal issues;

(ii) ascertain the names of all witnesses, including expert witnesses, parties intend to call and whose evidence they intend to rely on at proof;

(iii) consider the scope for use of affidavits and other documents in place of oral evidence;

(iv) consider whether sanction is sought for the employment of counsel;

(v) consider the reasonable estimate of time needed by each party for examination-in-chief, cross-examination and submissions;

(vi) order the lodging of joint minutes of agreement, affidavits, expert reports and any other documents within such period as the sheriff considers appropriate;

(vii) fix a diet of proof not less than 12 and not more than 16 weeks after the date of the preliminary hearing or any continuation thereof unless, on cause shown, a longer period is appropriate;

(viii) fix a pre-proof hearing not less than 6 and not more than 8 weeks before the diet of proof;

(ix) order answers to the statement referred to in rule 34A to be lodged within 14 days of the date of the preliminary hearing or any continuation thereof or such other period as the sheriff considers appropriate; and

(x) ascertain from the parties what, if any, expert evidence is required and consider the scope for joint instruction of a single expert

(2) The sheriff may, if satisfied that there is sufficient reason for doing so for the expeditious resolution of the cause, continue the preliminary hearing for such period or periods as he or she thinks fit.

(3) At the preliminary hearing the sheriff may—

(a) if he is not satisfied that the facts stated in the petition are supported by the documents lodged with it or by the reports of the curator *ad litem* and reporting officer, order the production of further documents; and

(b) make such other order as he considers appropriate for the expeditious progress of the case.

(4) The answers lodged under paragraph (1)(b)(ix) must be in numbered paragraphs and respond to the statement referred to in rule 34A.

List of witnesses etc.

35A. Not later than 7 days prior to the pre-proof hearing the parties shall lodge in process and intimate to all other parties—

(a) a list of the witnesses, including expert witnesses, they intend to call and whose evidence they intend to rely on at proof;

(b) all documents upon which they intend to rely at proof;

(c) a notice of agreed facts;

(d) a notice of disputed issues

Pre-proof hearing

36. (1) It is the duty of the parties to provide the sheriff with sufficient information to enable him to conduct the hearing as provided for in this rule.

(2) At the pre-proof hearing the sheriff must consider—

(a) the extent to which the parties have complied with any orders made by the sheriff under rule 35;

(b) the extent to which further information or orders are required in respect of matters referred to in rule 35;

(c) the state of preparation of the parties;

(d) the availability of witnesses;

(e) the nature of productions.

(2A) At the pre-proof hearing the sheriff must ascertain, so far as is reasonably practicable, whether the case is likely to proceed to proof on the date fixed for that purpose, whether the appropriate number of days have been allowed and if further days may be required.

(3) At the pre-proof hearing the sheriff may—

(a) discharge the proof and fix a new date for such proof;

(b) adjourn the pre-proof hearing;

(d) make such other order as he considers appropriate to secure the expeditious progress of the case including restricting the issues for proof and, on the motion of either party, on cause shown, or of the sheriff's own motion, excluding specified documents, reports and/or witnesses from proof .

Proof

37. (1) A proof shall be taken on the allocated days and parties shall adhere to the estimates provided under rule 35(1)(b)(v) or 36(2)(b), but the sheriff may adjourn the diet from time to time.

(2) Except where the sheriff otherwise directs, at the proof no witnesses other than those named on a witness list may be called to give evidence.

Pronouncement of decision

38. (1) At the conclusion of the proof the sheriff may—

(a) pronounce a decision; or

(b) reserve judgment.

(2) If the sheriff pronounces his decision at the end of the proof, he—

(a) must state briefly the grounds of his decision, including the reasons for his decision on any questions of law or of admissibility of evidence; and

(b) may, and if requested to do so by one of the parties must, append to the interlocutor a note setting out those matters and his findings in fact and law.

(3) If the sheriff pronounces his decision after reserving judgment, he must give to the sheriff clerk within 4 weeks of the conclusion of the proof—

(a) an interlocutor giving effect to his decision and incorporating findings in fact and law; and

(b) a note setting out the matters mentioned in paragraph (2)(a).

(4) The sheriff clerk must forthwith send copies of the documents mentioned in paragraph (2) or (3) to each of the parties.

(5) The sheriff principal may extend the period mentioned in paragraph (3) for such further period as he considers reasonable.

(6) Where the sheriff reserves judgment—

(a) the date of the interlocutor of the sheriff shall be the date on which it is received by the sheriff clerk; and

(b) the sheriff clerk shall enter that date in the interlocutor.

(7) If the question of expenses has been reserved the sheriff must deal with that issue within 21 days of the date of the interlocutor disposing of the merits of the application.

(8) In any case in which a serial number has been assigned in respect of the child's address under rule 43, or where the sheriff so directs, any document issued under this rule shall not disclose the child's address.

Final procedure

39. (1) This rule applies where a permanence order is granted.

(1A) The sheriff clerk must issue an extract of the order to the petitioner after—

(a) the expiry of the period within which an appeal may be made, if no appeal is made; or

(b) the appeal has been finally disposed of.

(1B) Where the court has also made an order under section 89(2) of the 2007 Act (revocation of compulsory supervision order on making of permanence order), the sheriff clerk must intimate the making of that order to the Principal Reporter.

(2) Where the permanence order includes provision granting authority for the child to be adopted the sheriff clerk must, after complying with

paragraphs (1A) and (IB) seal the process in an envelope marked "Confidential".

(3) The envelope referred to in paragraph (2) must not be unsealed by the sheriff clerk or any other person having control of the records of that or any court, and the process shall not be made accessible to any person for one hundred years after the date of the granting of the order except—

(a) to the person to whom the permanence order relates once he has attained the age of 16 years;

(b) to the sheriff clerk, on an application made to him by an adoption agency, with the consent of the person to whom the process relates, for the purpose only of ascertaining the name of the agency, if any, responsible for the placement of that person and informing the applicant of that name;

(c) to a person, on an application made by him to the sheriff setting forth the reasons for which access to the process is required;

(d) to a court, public authority or administrative board (whether in the United Kingdom or not) having power to authorise an adoption, on petition by it to the court which granted the original order requesting that information be made available from the process for the purpose of discharging its duties in considering an application for adoption and specifying the precise reasons for which access to the process is required; or

(e) to a person who is authorised by the Scottish Ministers to obtain information from the process for the purpose of such research as is intended to improve the working of adoption law and practice.

Variation of ancillary provisions in order

40. (1) An application under section 92(2) (application for variation of ancillary provisions) of the 2007 Act is to be made by minute in Form 16 in the process of the original application.

(2) A minute under paragraph (1) must contain—

(a) the name and address of the applicant;

(b) the applicant's relationship to and interest in the child;

(c) the name and address of the local authority on whose application the permanence order was granted;

(d) details of the original application;

(e) details of any other person affected by the order;

(f) the grounds on which variation is sought;

(g) details of whether the child is subject to a supervision requirement under section 70 of the 1995 Act;

(h) details of the order sought by the applicant.

(3) On the lodging of a minute under paragraph (1) the sheriff must order the applicant to intimate the minute to the petitioner in the original application, where it is not the applicant, to any other person affected by the order and to such other persons as the sheriff considers appropriate.

(4) A person to whom intimation is given under paragraph (3) may, within 14 days after the date on which intimation is made, lodge answers to the minute.

(5) The sheriff must, on the lodging of a minute under paragraph (1), appoint a curator *ad litem*.

(6) Where answers have been lodged under paragraph (4) the sheriff must order a hearing to be fixed.

(7) Where no answers have been lodged under paragraph (4) the sheriff may order a hearing to be fixed.

(8) Where the sheriff orders a hearing to be fixed under paragraph (6) or (7) he may also order a pre-proof hearing to be fixed not less than 2 and not more than 6 weeks before the hearing.

Rule 36 is to apply, with any necessary modifications, to any pre-proof hearing fixed under paragraph (8).

The sheriff shall order the applicant to intimate any hearing fixed under paragraph (6), (7) or (8) to the petitioner in the original application, where it is not the applicant, to any other person affected by the order and to such other persons as the sheriff considers appropriate.

A hearing fixed under this rule is to be taken continuously so far as possible but the sheriff may adjourn the diet from time to time.

Amendment of order to grant authority for child to be adopted

41. (1) An application under section 93(2) (amendment of order to include provision granting authority for child to be adopted) of the 2007 Act is to be made by minute in Form 17 in the process of the original application.

(2) A minute under paragraph (1) must contain—

(a) the name and address of the applicant;

(b) details of the original application;

(c) details of the following matters—

(i) whether the child has been, or is likely to be, placed for adoption;

(ii) whether each parent or guardian of the child understands what the effect of making an adoption order would be and consents to the making of such an order in relation to the child, or the grounds on which such consent should be dispensed with;

(iii) the child's religious persuasion, racial origin and cultural and linguistic background;

(iv) whether the child is subject to a supervision requirement under section 70 of the 1995 Act;

(v) the likely effect on the child of the making of the order.

(3) On the lodging of a minute under paragraph (1)—

(a) the sheriff clerk must fix a date for a preliminary hearing not less than 6 and not more than 8 weeks after the date of lodging the application;

(b) the applicant must send a copy of the minute along with a notice of intimation in Form 18 to every person who can be found and whose consent to the making of the order is required to be given or dispensed with under the 2007 Act;

(c) the applicant must send a copy of the minute along with a notice of intimation in Form 19 to the father of the child if he does not have, and never has had, parental responsibilities in relation to the child;

(d) the sheriff may order the applicant to intimate the minute to such other persons as he considers appropriate;

(e) the sheriff must appoint a curator *ad litem* and reporting officer and the same person may be appointed as curator *ad litem* and reporting officer if the sheriff considers that doing so is appropriate in the circumstances.

(4) A notice of intimation under paragraph (3)(b) must state the following matters:—

(a) that an application has been made;

(b) the date on which, and place where, the preliminary hearing will be heard;

(c) the fact that the person is entitled to be heard on the application;

(d) the fact that, unless the person wishes, or the court requires, the person need not attend the hearing.

(5) A notice of intimation under paragraph (3)(c) must state the matters mentioned in paragraph (4)(a) and (b).

(6) The minuter on making intimation shall complete a certificate of intimation in Form 14.

(7) Rules 34 to 39 are to apply, with any necessary modifications, to an application under this rule as they apply to an application under rule 31.

Revocation

42. (1) An application under section 98(1) of the 2007 Act for revocation of a permanence order shall—

(a) be made by minute in Form 20 in the process of the original application; and

(b) specify detailed proposals for the future welfare of the child.

(2) A minute under paragraph (1) must contain—

(a) the name and address of the applicant;

(b) the applicant's relationship to and interest in the child;

(c) the name and address of the local authority on whose application the permanence order was granted;

(d) details of the original application;

(e) details of any other person affected by the order;

(f) the grounds on which revocation is sought;

(g) details of whether the child is subject to a supervision requirement under section 70 of the 1995 Act;

(h) details of the order sought by the applicant.

(3) On the lodging of a minute under paragraph (1), the sheriff must order the applicant to intimate the minute to the petitioner in the original application, where it is not the applicant, to any other person affected by the order and to such other persons as he considers appropriate.

(4) Any person to whom intimation has been given under paragraph (3) may, within 14 days after the date on which intimation is made, lodge answers to the minute.

(5) The sheriff must, on the lodging of a minute under paragraph (1), appoint a curator *ad litem*.

(6) Where answers have been lodged under paragraph (4), the sheriff—

(a) must order a hearing to be fixed; and

(b) may order the relevant local authority to submit a report to him.

(7) Where no answers have been lodged under paragraph (4) the sheriff may—

(a) order the relevant local authority to submit a report to him;

(b) order a hearing to be fixed;

(c) order both such a report and such a hearing.

(8) Where the sheriff orders a hearing to be fixed under paragraph (6) or (7) he may also order a pre-proof hearing to be fixed not less than 2 and not more than 6 weeks before the hearing.

(9) Rule 36 is to apply, with any necessary modifications, to any pre-proof hearing fixed under paragraph (8).

(10) The sheriff shall order the applicant to intimate any hearing fixed under paragraph (6), (7) or (8) to the petitioner in the original application, where it is not the applicant, to any other person affected by the order and to such other persons as the sheriff considers appropriate.

(11) A hearing fixed under this rule is to be taken continuously so far as possible but the sheriff may adjourn the diet from time to time.

(12) An order made in respect of an application under paragraph (1) may specify the person—

(a) on whom parental responsibilities are imposed in consequence of the making of the order; and

(b) to whom parental rights are given in consequence of the making of the order.

Protection of address of child

43. (1) Where an applicant under this Chapter wishes to prevent the address of the child being disclosed to any person whose consent to the making of an order is required, the applicant may apply to the sheriff clerk for a serial number to be assigned for that purpose.

(2) On receipt of an application under paragraph (1) the sheriff clerk must—

(a) assign a serial number in respect of the child's address; and

(b) enter a note of the number opposite the child's address in a register of serial numbers.

(3) The contents of the register of serial numbers and the addresses of the children to whom each number relates shall be treated as confidential by the sheriff clerk and are not to be disclosed to any person other than the sheriff.

(4) Where a serial number has been assigned under paragraph (2), any form of consent to a permanence order—

(a) must refer to the child's address by means of the serial number assigned to it; and

(b) must specify the year in which and the court by which the serial number was assigned.

Duties of reporting officer and curator *ad litem*

44. (1) The other duties of a reporting officer appointed under this Chapter, other than under rule 32(3), which are prescribed for the purposes of section 108(1)(b) of the 2007 Act are—

(a) to ascertain the whereabouts of all persons whose consent to the making of an adoption order in respect of the child is required;

(b) to ascertain whether there is any person other than those mentioned in the petition or minute, as the case may be, upon whom notice of the application should be served;

(c) in the case of each person whose consent to the making of an adoption order is required or may be dispensed with, to—

(i) ascertain whether that person understands what the effect of making an adoption order would be;

(ii) ascertain whether alternatives to adoption have been discussed with that person;

(iia) ascertain whether that person consents to the making of an adoption order;

(iii) confirm that that person understands that he may withdraw his consent at any time before an order is made;

(d) to confirm that each parent or guardian of the child who can be found is aware that he may apply to the court for—

(i) variation of the ancillary provisions in the permanence order under section 92 of the 2007 Act; and

(ii) revocation of a permanence order under section 98 of the 2007 Act,and of the appropriate procedure for these applications.

(e) to report in writing on the matters mentioned in subparagraphs (a) to (d) to the sheriff within 4 weeks from date of interlocutor appointing the reporting officer, or within such other period as the sheriff in his discretion may allow.

(2) References in paragraph (1) to consent are to consent within the meaning of section 83(1)(c), 84(1) or 93(3) of the 2007 Act as the case may be.

(3) A curator *ad litem* appointed under this Chapter must—

(a) have regard to safeguarding the interests of the child as his paramount duty;

(b) inquire, so far as he considers necessary into the facts and circumstances stated in the petition or minute, as the case may be, and in any report lodged under rule 31(2)(b);

(c) where appropriate, establish the child's religious persuasion, racial origin and cultural and linguistic background;

(d) where appropriate, establish whether the order is likely to safeguard and promote the welfare of the child throughout childhood;

(e) ascertain whether the child is subject to a supervision requirement under section 70 of the 1995 Act;

(f) ascertain from the child whether he wishes to express a view and, where the child indicates his wish to express a view, ascertain that view;

(g) ascertain the likely effect on the child of the making of the order;

(h) where appropriate, ascertain whether it would be better for the child that the order be made than that it should not be made;

(i) where appropriate, ascertain whether it would be better for the child if the court were to grant authority for the child to be adopted than if it were not to grant such authority;

(ii) where appropriate, ascertain whether the child has been, or is likely to be, placed for adoption.

(4) Subject to paragraph (5) the curator *ad litem* must report in writing on the matters mentioned in paragraph (3) to the sheriff within 4 weeks from the date of the interlocutor appointing the curator, or within such other period as the sheriff in his discretion may allow.

(5) Subject to any order made by the sheriff under rule 46(1)(a) the views of the child ascertained in terms of paragraph (3)(f) may, if the curator *ad litem* considers appropriate, be conveyed to the sheriff orally.

Consents

45. (1) The consent of a parent or guardian required by section 83(1)(c) or 93(3) of the 2007 Act is to be in Form 21.

(2) The consent of the child required under section 84(1) of the 2007 Act is to be in Form 22.

(3) A form of consent mentioned in paragraph (1) or (2) must be witnessed—

(a) where it is executed in Scotland, by the reporting officer appointed under this Chapter;

(b) where it is executed outwith Scotland but within the United Kingdom, by a justice of the peace or commissioner for oaths; or

(c) where it is executed outwith the United Kingdom—

(i) if the person who executes the form is serving in Her Majesty's forces, by an officer holding a commission in any of those forces; or

(ii) in any other case, by a British diplomatic or consular official or any person authorised to administer an oath or affirmation under the law of the place where the consent is executed.

Procedure where child wishes to express a view

46. (1) Where a child has indicated his wish to express his views the sheriff, without prejudice to rule 44(3)(f)—

(a) may order such procedural steps to be taken as he considers appropriate to ascertain the views of that child; and

(b) must not make an order under this Chapter unless an opportunity has been given for the views of that child to be obtained or heard.

(2) Where the views of a child, whether obtained under this rule or under rule 44, have been recorded in writing, the sheriff may direct that such a written record is to—

(a) be sealed in a envelope marked "Views of the child – confidential";

(b) be available to a sheriff only;

(c) not be opened by any person other than a sheriff; and

(d) not form a borrowable part of the process.

Confidentiality

47. (1) Unless the sheriff otherwise directs, all documents lodged in process including the reports by the curator *ad litem* and reporting officer shall be available only to the sheriff, the curator *ad litem*, the reporting officer and the parties; and such documents must be treated as confidential by any persons involved in, or a party to, the proceedings and by the sheriff clerk.

(2) The reporting officer and the curator *ad litem*—

(a) must treat all information obtained in the exercise of their duties as confidential; and

(b) must not disclose any such information to any person unless disclosure of such information is necessary for the purpose of their duties.

(3) This rule is subject to rule 46 and rule 51.

Procedure where leave of court required

48. (1) Where leave of the court is required under section 94(4) or 98(2)(b) of the 2007 Act before an application for variation or revocation of a permanence order may be made, the applicant must lodge along with the minute a written application in the form of a letter addressed to the sheriff clerk stating—

(a) the grounds on which leave is sought; and

(b) whether or not the applicant has applied for legal aid.

(2) Where the applicant has applied for legal aid he must also lodge along with the minute written confirmation from the Scottish Legal Aid Board that it has determined, under regulation 7(2)(b) of the Civil Legal Aid (Scotland) Regulations 2002 that notification of the application should be dispensed with or postponed pending the making by the sheriff of an order for intimation under paragraph (4)(b).

(3) Subject to paragraph (4)(b), an application under paragraph (1) shall not be served or intimated to any party.

(4) The sheriff shall consider an application under paragraph (1) without hearing the applicant and may—

(a) refuse the application and pronounce an interlocutor accordingly; or

(b) if he is minded to grant the application order the applicant—

(i) to intimate the application to such persons as the sheriff considers appropriate; and

(ii) to lodge a certificate of intimation in, as near as may be, Form 7.

(5) If any person who receives intimation of an application under paragraph (4)(b) wishes to be heard he shall notify the sheriff clerk in writing within 14 days of receipt of intimation of the application.

(6) On receipt of the notification under paragraph (5) the sheriff clerk shall fix a hearing and intimate the date of the hearing to the parties.

Transfer of process

49. (1) Where an application under rule 40, 41 or 42 is made in a sheriff court other than the sheriff court in which the process relating to the permanence order is held—

(a) the minute of application must contain averments as to the sheriff court in which the process relating to the permanence order is held;

(b) the sheriff clerk with whom the application is lodged must notify the sheriff clerk of the sheriff court in which the process relating to the permanence order is held; and

(c) the sheriff clerk of the sheriff court in which the process relating to the permanence order is held must, not later than 4 working days after receipt of such notification transfer that process to the sheriff clerk of the sheriff court in which the application is made.

(2) For the purposes of paragraph (1), the sheriff court in which the process relating to the order is held is the sheriff court in which the permanence order was granted or, where the process has been transferred

under that paragraph, the last sheriff court to which the process has been transferred.

(3) A failure of the sheriff clerk to comply with paragraph (1) does not invalidate the application.

Intimation to Principal Reporter

50. Where an application under this Chapter is made in respect of a child whose case has been referred to a children's hearing or who is subject to a supervision requirement under the 1995 Act, the sheriff clerk shall intimate the fact that the application has been made to the Principal Reporter.

Report of children's hearing

51. (1) This rule applies where the sheriff is given a report from a children's hearing under section 95(2) of the 2007 Act.

(1A) The sheriff clerk shall lodge in the process of the application—

(a) the report, and

(b) where paragraph (1C) applies, the documents referred to in that paragraph.

(1B) Subject to paragraph (1D), the sheriff clerk shall send a copy of the report together with a notice in Form 23 to—

(a) the parties to the application;

(b) any relevant person in relation to the child; and

(c) such other person as the sheriff considers appropriate.

(1C) This paragraph, and paragraphs (1D) and (1E) apply where, pursuant to rule 77(7) of the Children's Hearings (Scotland) Act 2011 (Rules of Procedure in Children's Hearings) Rules 2013(5), the sheriff is given, in addition to the report referred to in paragraph (1)—

(a) a redacted report, and

(b) details of the children's hearing's determination of a non-disclosure request.

(1D) The sheriff shall, having regard to the details referred to in paragraph (1C)(b), determine in respect of each person referred to in paragraph (1B) whether that persons to be sent a copy of the redacted report in place of a copy of the report, and paragraph (1B) shall apply accordingly.

(1E) Unless the sheriff otherwise directs, the report lodged in the process shall not be available to any person to whom a copy of the redacted report has been sent pursuant to paragraph (1D).

(2) Any person who receives notice under paragraph (1B) and who wishes to oppose the proposals of the children's hearing must lodge a form of response in Form 24 within 7 days of the date notice was given.

(3) Thereafter the sheriff shall consider the report and any form of response lodged under paragraph (2) and decide whether to refer the child's case to the Principal Reporter as mentioned in section 96(3) of the 2007 Act.

(4) Where the sheriff decides to refer the child's case to the Principal Reporter as mentioned in section 96(3) of the 2007 Act, he shall pronounce an order to this effect which shall narrate in terms that he is referring the child's case to the Principal Reporter as mentioned in that provision.

(5) Where the sheriff decides not to refer the child's case to the Principal Reporter, he may nevertheless make such other order he considers appropriate for the expeditious progress of the case.

(6) In order to assist him to decide what to do under paragraph (3), the sheriff may order the holding of a hearing.

(7) If the sheriff so decides, he shall fix a date for the hearing which shall be not more than 7 days after the date of the order.

(8) The sheriff clerk shall intimate any hearing under paragraph (6) to—

(a) the parties to the application;

(b) any person who lodged a form of response under paragraph (2);

(c) any relevant person in relation to the child within the meaning given by section 93(2) of the 1995 Act; and

(d) such other person as the sheriff considers appropriate.

(9) The sheriff may allow a continuation of a hearing under paragraph (6) on two occasions only, each for a period not exceeding 14 days.

(10) After the sheriff has made his decision under paragraph (3), the sheriff clerk shall send a notice in Form 25 to the Principal Reporter.

Interim orders

52. (1) An application for an interim order under section 97 of the 2007 Act is to be made by motion.

(2) Chapter 15 of the Ordinary Cause Rules shall apply, with any necessary modifications, to a motion under this rule as it applies to a motion under the Ordinary Cause Rules.

SUBJECT INDEX

'A Practical Guide to Hoarding and Mental Health for Housing Lawyers' by Rachel Coyle
'A Practical Guide to Psychiatric Claims in Personal Injury – 2nd Edition' by Liam Ryan
'Stephens on Contractual Indemnities' by Richard Stephens
'A Practical Guide to the EU Succession Regulation' by Richard Frimston
'A Practical Guide to Solicitor and Client Costs – 2nd Edition' by Robin Dunne
'Constructive Dismissal – Practice Pointers and Principles' by Benjimin Burgher
'A Practical Guide to Religion and Belief Discrimination Claims in the Workplace' by Kashif Ali
'A Practical Guide to the Law of Medical Treatment Decisions' by Ben Troke
'Fundamental Dishonesty and QOCS in Personal Injury Proceedings: Law and Practice' by Jake Rowley
'A Practical Guide to the Law in Relation to School Exclusions' by Charlotte Hadfield & Alice de Coverley
'A Practical Guide to Divorce for the Silver Separators' by Karin Walker
'The Right to be Forgotten – The Law and Practical Issues' by Melissa Stock
'A Practical Guide to Planning Law and Rights of Way in National Parks, the Broads and AONBs' by James Maurici QC, James Neill et al
'A Practical Guide to Election Law' by Tom Tabori
'A Practical Guide to the Law in Relation to Surrogacy' by Andrew Powell
'A Practical Guide to Claims Arising from Fatal Accidents – 2nd Edition' by James Patience
'A Practical Guide to the Ownership of Employee Inventions – From Entitlement to Compensation' by James Tumbridge & Ashley Roughton
'A Practical Guide to Asbestos Claims' by Jonathan Owen & Gareth McAloon
'A Practical Guide to Stamp Duty Land Tax in England and Northern Ireland' by Suzanne O'Hara
'A Practical Guide to the Law of Farming Partnerships' by Philip Whitcomb
'Covid-19, Homeworking and the Law – The Essential Guide to Employment and GDPR Issues' by Forbes Solicitors
'Covid-19 and Criminal Law – The Essential Guide' by Ramya Nagesh
'Covid-19 and Family Law in England and Wales – The Essential Guide' by Safda Mahmood

'A Practical Guide to the Law of Unlawful Eviction and Harassment – 2nd Edition' by Stephanie Lovegrove
'Covid-19, Brexit and the Law of Commercial Leases – The Essential Guide' by Mark Shelton
'A Practical Guide to Costs in Personal Injury Claims – 2nd Edition' by Matthew Hoe
'A Practical Guide to the General Data Protection Regulation (GDPR) – 2nd Edition' by Keith Markham
'Ellis on Credit Hire – Sixth Edition' by Aidan Ellis & Tim Kevan
'A Practical Guide to Working with Litigants in Person and McKenzie Friends in Family Cases' by Stuart Barlow
'Protecting Unregistered Brands: A Practical Guide to the Law of Passing Off' by Lorna Brazell
'A Practical Guide to Secondary Liability and Joint Enterprise Post-Jogee' by Joanne Cecil & James Mehigan
'A Practical Guide to the Pre-Action RTA Claims Protocol for Personal Injury Lawyers' by Antonia Ford
'A Practical Guide to Neighbour Disputes and the Law' by Alexander Walsh
'A Practical Guide to Forfeiture of Leases' by Mark Shelton
'A Practical Guide to Coercive Control for Legal Practitioners and Victims' by Rachel Horman
'A Practical Guide to Rights Over Airspace and Subsoil' by Daniel Gatty
'Tackling Disclosure in the Criminal Courts – A Practitioner's Guide' by Narita Bahra QC & Don Ramble
'A Practical Guide to the Law of Driverless Cars – Second Edition' by Alex Glassbrook, Emma Northey & Scarlett Milligan
'A Practical Guide to TOLATA Claims' by Greg Williams
'A Practical Guide to Elderly Law – 2nd Edition' by Justin Patten
'A Practical Guide to Responding to Housing Disrepair and Unfitness Claims' by Iain Wightwick
'A Practical Guide to the Construction and Rectification of Wills and Trust Instruments' by Edward Hewitt
'A Practical Guide to the Law of Bullying and Harassment in the Workplace' by Philip Hyland
'How to Be a Freelance Solicitor: A Practical Guide to the SRA-Regulated Freelance Solicitor Model' by Paul Bennett

'A Practical Guide to Prison Injury Claims' by Malcolm Johnson
'A Practical Guide to the Small Claims Track - 2nd Edition' by Dominic Bright
'A Practical Guide to Advising Clients at the Police Station' by Colin Stephen McKeown-Beaumont
'A Practical Guide to Antisocial Behaviour Injunctions' by Iain Wightwick
'Practical Mediation: A Guide for Mediators, Advocates, Advisers, Lawyers, and Students in Civil, Commercial, Business, Property, Workplace, and Employment Cases' by Jonathan Dingle with John Sephton
'The Mini-Pupillage Workbook' by David Boyle
'A Practical Guide to Crofting Law' by Brian Inkster
'A Practical Guide to Spousal Maintenance' by Liz Cowell
'A Practical Guide to the Law of Domain Names and Cybersquatting' by Andrew Clemson
'A Practical Guide to the Law of Gender Pay Gap Reporting' by Harini Iyengar
'A Practical Guide to the Rights of Grandparents in Children Proceedings' by Stuart Barlow
'NHS Whistleblowing and the Law' by Joseph England
'Employment Law and the Gig Economy' by Nigel Mackay & Annie Powell
'A Practical Guide to Noise Induced Hearing Loss (NIHL) Claims' by Andrew Mckie, Ian Skeate, Gareth McAloon
'An Introduction to Beauty Negligence Claims – A Practical Guide for the Personal Injury Practitioner' by Greg Almond
'Intercompany Agreements for Transfer Pricing Compliance' by Paul Sutton
'Zen and the Art of Mediation' by Martin Plowman
'A Practical Guide to the SRA Principles, Individual and Law Firm Codes of Conduct 2019 – What Every Law Firm Needs to Know' by Paul Bennett
'A Practical Guide to Adoption for Family Lawyers' by Graham Pegg
'A Practical Guide to Industrial Disease Claims' by Andrew Mckie & Ian Skeate
'A Practical Guide to Redundancy' by Philip Hyland
'A Practical Guide to Vicarious Liability' by Mariel Irvine
'A Practical Guide to Applications for Landlord's Consent and Variation of Leases' by Mark Shelton
'A Practical Guide to Relief from Sanctions Post-Mitchell and Denton' by Peter Causton

‘A Practical Guide to Equity Release for Advisors’ by Paul Sams
‘A Practical Guide to Financial Services Claims’ by Chris Hegarty
‘The Law of Houses in Multiple Occupation: A Practical Guide to HMO Proceedings’ by Julian Hunt
‘Occupiers, Highways and Defective Premises Claims: A Practical Guide Post-Jackson – 2nd Edition’ by Andrew Mckie
‘A Practical Guide to Financial Ombudsman Service Claims’ by Adam Temple & Robert Scrivenor
'A Practical Guide to Advising Schools on Employment Law' by Jonathan Holden
‘A Practical Guide to Running Housing Disrepair and Cavity Wall Claims: 2nd Edition’ by Andrew Mckie & Ian Skeate
‘A Practical Guide to Holiday Sickness Claims – 2nd Edition’ by Andrew Mckie & Ian Skeate
‘Arguments and Tactics for Personal Injury and Clinical Negligence Claims’ by Dorian Williams
‘A Practical Guide to Drone Law’ by Rufus Ballaster, Andrew Firman, Eleanor Clot
‘A Practical Guide to Compliance for Personal Injury Firms Working With Claims Management Companies’ by Paul Bennett
‘RTA Allegations of Fraud in a Post-Jackson Era: The Handbook – 2nd Edition’ by Andrew Mckie
‘RTA Personal Injury Claims: A Practical Guide Post-Jackson’ by Andrew Mckie
‘On Experts: CPR35 for Lawyers and Experts’ by David Boyle
‘An Introduction to Personal Injury Law’ by David Boyle

These books and more are available to order online direct from the publisher at www.lawbriefpublishing.com, where you can also read free sample chapters. For any queries, contact us on 0844 587 2383 or mail@lawbriefpublishing.com.

Our books are also usually in stock at www.amazon.co.uk with free next day delivery for Prime members, and at good legal bookshops such as Wildy & Sons.

We are regularly launching new books in our series of practical day-to-day practitioners' guides. Visit our website and join our free newsletter to be kept informed and to receive special offers, free chapters, etc.

You can also follow us on Twitter at www.twitter.com/lawbriefpub.

www.ingramcontent.com/pod-product-compliance
Lightning Source LLC
LaVergne TN
LVHW052314200926
848481LV00002B/561
9781914608995